Cynthia Ann Parker

CYNTHIA ANN PARKER

Cynthia Ann Parker

by

Grace Jackson

THE NAYLOR COMPANY
The Publishers of the Southwest - - San Antonio, Texas

A PATHFINDER BOOK REPRINT EDITION
Complete and Unabridged

Printed in the United States of America

ISBN: 979-8-8691-1323-8

Dedicated

to

Joe O. Naylor

Lover of Southwest history and culture, who inspired me to write this story of Cynthia Ann Parker

Foreword

The story of Cynthia Ann Parker is one of adventure, romance, and pathos, depicting the spirit of the American way of life. In 1757, John Parker was born in Virginia, and his life is typical of the pioneer faith which has been the inheritance of those living today. Leaving Virginia in 1785, he crossed the distance of 3500 miles only to die at the hand of the Comanche Indians in 1836. John Parker's son, Silas, was the father of Cynthia Ann and he accompanied the elder Parker to the country of southeast Texas where they settled and built Fort Parker.

Rejoicing over the victory of the Battle of San Jacinto on the evening of May 18, 1836, they rested from their labors and disbanded the rangers who had been at the fort for their protection. On May 19, the Comanche Indians struck, killing the men in the stockade and taking Cynthia Ann and her brother John captive. The Comanches gave her a new name, Preloch, when she was taken captive. Cynthia Ann was nine years old when she last saw her mother, and for twenty-four long years she lived with the Indians of the plains.

She married Peta Nocona and became a Comanche princess, following him in his raids against the white people. She adopted their habits and customs and bore him three children.

At the Battle of Pease river, in 1860, she was captured

by the white soldiers at the location where they killed her Indian chief, Peta Nocona. Taken by Captain Ross back to Camp Cooper to the white people, she could not speak English; nor did she recognize her uncle Isaac Parker who came to find her. Her bewildered mind finally awoke; she must have heard a faint echo of her own dead mother's voice crying "Cynthia Ann." The scowl on her face faded, and, falteringly and brokenly, she framed the forgotten words "Cynthia - me - Cynthia" and pressed her hand against her heart.

She was returned to her white relatives at the age of thirty-four and was sad and lonely, for her constant association with the Indians had changed her habits, ways and customs. She tried to run away with her little girl, Prairie Flower or Tecks Ann, who had been captured with her. She mourned the loss of her two boys, Pecos and Quanah, fearing they had perished on the prairie. The child, Prairie Flower, did not live long in her white captivity, and grief-stricken Cynthia Ann passed away in 1864.

Quanah, her Indian son, lived however to become a famous Comanche chief. He advertised for a picture of his mother in the Fort Worth Gazette. Captain Ross found and gave him the only picture of his mother that is known to exist. He requested that his mother's body be brought to Cache, Oklahoma, where he was buried beside the grave of his mother. Both graves are now in Fort Sill, where they were moved by the government.

Acknowledgments

The author wishes to express her appreciation for the kindness and benefits received in reproducing the story of Cynthia Ann Parker to the following: Bureau of American Ethnology at the Smithsonian Institute, Washington, D.C., for photographs: Microfilm Service of the Southern Methodist University; William Allen Ward, Dallas Journal (Oct. 4, 1935); T. J. Cates of Ben Wheeler, Texas; R. N. Richardson of Hardin Simmons; Ralph Selle; Pauline Buck Hohes; James T. De Shields; Roberts Coldwater Carter; Wentworth Manning; Carl Rister, and a host of others whose material I have read and from which information was gleaned. Also I want to thank those who have read the manuscript and the descendants of Cynthia Ann and Quanah Parker, whom I have met.

Contents

Ballad of Cynthia Ann Parker

by

William Allen Ward

The wagon train is in the gulch and smoke is on the hill.
The Kiowa in silence stands, then calls the tribe to kill.

> The soul of Cynthia is riding again,
> Nocona is leading the way;
> They're racing across gray hills,
> For soon it will be day
>
> Over the butte in the valley below
> Is the white man's wagon train;
> But Cynthia is a Chieftain's wife —
> She can never be white again.
>
> Peta Nocona with pagan heart
> Thrills to the pale maid's love.
> Across the Brazos they ride again,
> While the moon looks down from above.
>
> Again they will fight the invaders,
> The Paleface from the timbered land,
> The Comanche, the Kiowa claim
> The Prairie and its shifting sand.

The wagon train is in the gulch and smoke is on the hill.
The Kiowa in silence stands, then calls the tribe to kill.

— *Dallas Journal*
Oct. 4, 1935

xii

CHAPTER I

Home from the Wars

A GROUP OF WAR-WEARY PATRIOTS had emptied their powder horns and were trudging down the trails toward the hills of home. They had left Virginia more than two years before, for they had gone to fight the British. After the victory of Yorktown, the peace had been signed and the militia had been disbanded. This company of young men had started for home. The countryside was not new to John Parker, for, as a young man, he had fought the Indians and helped his parents build a home there.

These parts of Virginia were sparsely settled, but in these mountains, in Culpeper County, John was born in 1757. He had lived a quiet life until the American colonies began their war for independence against England. John was a lad of nineteen when he left his parents and his girl sweetheart, Sallie White, and went to the aid of his country. As he walked home, tall and handsome in his buff and blue worn regimentals, he wondered if Sally had waited for him to return. Sally was a tall frontier girl whose parents had lived near the Parker land. John Parker was welcomed home by his family and sweetheart and busy days followed. There were new wardrobes for John, and soon he and Sallie were married at his parents' home. It was out of this rock that the Parker fame was hewn.

Culpeper County, Virginia. In April of 1781, a first son was born to John and Sally Parker, and they named him Daniel. Because both John and Sally were of the Baptist faith, they felt that their children should have names of men who had lived in Biblical times, and whose lives measured up to their religious beliefs. Thus, all of their sons were named for men who were in the Bible. The next son, they named John, and then Isaac arrived and was given the Old Testament patriarch's name.

The colony of Virginia in these years was still new, and the experiences with the red man were still very real with these new settlers. They still sharpened their hunting knives and put their rifles in order. The cruel, hard years at the close of the revolution brought hardships that were al - most unbearable to the struggling few. God, in his providence, used it to put metal into the sinews of these people for their future life in the West. The suffering economics of the trodden-down colonists caused them to seek their fortunes in the cotton fields of Georgia. They felt sure that the English trade would increase as the fields of cotton were planted. They thought they could turn to these fluffy white pods as a medium of trade between their poverty-stricken lands and the countries of Europe.

Elbert County, Georgia. One afternoon, the wagons and horses drove up to transport the Parker family from Virginia to Georgia. It was the ambition of John Parker that sent him trekking south with his family. The roads were very poor. From Culpeper, they took the secondary road to Orange, then Charlottesville and on to the place called Lynch's Ferry. From Lynch's Ferry they moved slowly down to Salem. From Salem they journeyed to the town of Charlotte in North Carolina where there was a main road, and the highway was completed through Camden to Augusta, Georgia. From Augusta there was an old secondary road up to Elbert County. They settled on a farm on the Savannah River, and life was much the same in this colony except that they had Negroes to do much of the manual labor on the small farm. While in Georgia, John Parker was made an elder in his church, and from this time on was called by the name, "Elder John." During this stay in Georgia, James Parker was born, the fourth son of John and Sallie. But the call of the West was still strong, and as civilization pushed to their countryside in Georgia, the urge to leave and go West was in the heart of Elder John. Rumors were reaching Georgia of the opportunities in beautiful Tennessee. He decided to take his family over the mountains to this new country of opportunity.

Bedford County, Tennessee. The family reached Petersburg in the present Elbert County which was on the Savannah River and not far from their home. The river divided here into the Tugaloo and the Broad River. The Parkers had to go up the Broad River and cross the lower Cherokee country to the town of Dahlonega, at the head of the Etowah River. Here they crossed in the middle of Cherokee country across the river Coosa to the town of Ustanali. From there they soon came to the Tennessee River in the Chickamauga territory. They took the Nickajack Trail from Nickajack to below Nashville in Bedford County. As the group moved from Georgia to Tennessee, John conducted the church services wherever they had a small band of believers. Every Lord's day there was preaching and singing, with Elder John acting as the leader. Thus, John Parker lived for twelve years in Bedford County, Tennessee. He always found a river, so he settled on the Duck River where there was plenty of water for family and stock. During these years there were born two more sons, Silas M. and Benjamin Parker. Silas is the father of Cynthia Ann Parker, the heroine of this story. Benjamin was the youngest and last son of Elder John, and was named after the Bible character who was the youngest son of the Patriarch Isaac.

The family always stayed together, and when Elder John moved, all the sons accompanied him, bringing their wives and children with the clan. There were many streams to ford, steep banks to climb. They worked their way through roadless swamps, until they reached their destination. Tennessee was covered with luscious timber, and game was plentiful. The streams were alive with fish. The Parker family had grown large in number. They entertained trappers and traders from the territory of Illinois, which was a part of the Louisiana Purchase (1803). Through these travelers, they heard of the dark, fallow soil that produced in abundance.

The War of 1812 caused a decided difference in the life of the Parker family. Daniel, the oldest boy, and Isaac, the next brother, marched off to join the 39th Regiment. They were not sent to fight the British, but were assigned to a battalion whose duty was to hold the Creek Indians that were allied with the English. Under a treaty made with the colonists, the Creeks had possession of a large territory. The white settlers had violated this treaty. The British supplied the Creeks with arms, and the Indian braves rose under a half-breed whose name was Bill Weathersford. Settlers fled to stockades and forts for safety, but this half-breed fell upon them and killed 400 white people. Thus, with 2500 Tennessee militia, General Andrew Jackson went after this man. Daniel and Isaac fought in the Battle of Horseshoe Bend on the Tallapoosa River, which was fifty-five miles south of Fort Strother. It was here that Sam Houston led the fight and fell wounded. The Parker brothers may have helped make the litter of sapling poles upon which he was carried back to Tennessee. The brothers returned home victorious. The settlers were still streaming into Tennessee just as the Parkers had done. They wanted land, and this new territory was mostly owned by the Indians.

Crawford County, Illinois. In the year 1814, Elder John was fifty-seven, but the lure of travel still burned in his blood. The pioneer, with wagons and belongings, started for the state of Illinois. The family now consisted of six sons — Daniel, John, Isaac, James, Silas, and Benjamin. They were all married but the youngest son, Benjamin. These young men felt the strong call of the West, and thus they went along with the father. They followed the Cumberland River north from Tennessee to the Ohio. There they crossed and followed the Ohio, bearing to the right to the Wabash, and north to Crawford County, Illinois. They built their log cabins and planted grain and vegetables, waiting for the winter to come. The Parker clan settled down in Illinois for a few years. In Crawford County the blessed event took place, for Cynthia Ann Parker was born.

Grandfather John was seventy, but still active in the affairs of the frontier community. His son Silas had married a lovely frontier girl named Lucy Duty, and James had married her sister, Martha Duty. This was now the year 1827. Daniel, the elder son, was fifty-two, and had begun to take over the leadership of the clan. He had married Martha Dixon, and seven children were born to this union. Isaac was forty years old and was the father of eight children. It was into this sturdy stock of Americans that lovely Cynthia Ann was born in 1827.

The dangers of the frontier settlement were many, but the greatest foe was a fever which the children seemed to contract. Isaac lost three of his children by this sickness, and he was determined to leave this country. Three years later, in 1830, Cynthia Ann had a baby brother. They named him John. He was Cynthia Ann's pride and joy. She played with him on the earthen floor as her mother worked in the cabin preparing food and clothing for her growing family. Ft. Le Mott in Crawford County, Illinois, in what is now Palestine, was in a swampy river country, and there was also some danger from the Delaware Indians in nearby Missouri. It was during this time in Illinois that the sad news came of the death of their brother John, killed while fighting the Indians near Cape Girardeau, Missouri. Thus, after about fifteen years in Illinois, from 1817-1832, the Parker family decided to move to Texas. Both James and Daniel had heard about the great Mexican province of Texas and of Stephen Austin's colony, where every married man could have 4,600 acres free land in that vast domain. Daniel Parker, the leader of the family, now decided to make a trip to Texas for two purposes: to find land for the Parkers to settle on, and to organize a Baptist church in this new land. In the fall of 1830, James and Daniel left Illinois to search out the country, arriving in Feb., 1831. After spending a few months on the Angelina River, the Colorado, and the Brazos, they returned to Illinois with their news of the new country of Texas.

Elder Daniel Parker was anxious to start his church, but the laws of Texas forbade him to do this. He had become well-known as the first propounder and advocate of the "Two Seeds" doctrine. He therefore organized his church in Illinois and brought the forty members to Texas with him. His six families, with their sons and children, made up the bulk of his congregation.

Limestone County, Texas. In 1832, the entire membership of the Parker family was ready to move, since they always went together. They had twenty-four ox-drawn wagons and they moved not only the Parker clan, but the Baptist church with them. Silas and Lucy put all their belongings in one of the wagons with the three babies: Cynthia Ann, now five; John, who was two; and the baby, who had been born just a few months before. It was a long, weary trip, and took several months. With the Parkers came some other families whose names are recorded as the Browns, Kennedys, Jourdans, Greenwoods, Lagos, the Bennetts, and others. With John Parker were six sons: Daniel, Isaac, James, Silas, Joseph A., and Benjamin. Then Daniel Parker had five sons: Dickson, Daniel, Benjamin, Isaac and Kalab, and two sons-in-law, Joseph Kennedy and Ruben Brown.

The process of making and breaking camp became soon a familiar sight to the little five-year-old Cynthia Ann. Fifteen, seventeen, even twenty miles a day was not too much over the pleasant grassy flats of Missouri. They reached St. Louis and bought supplies for the journey south. They followed the path of the Mississippi and found plenty of wild game and water for their stock. They lived well on wild turkey, wild pigeon and antelope meat; and while they stopped at night, the men would fish in the streams. It was less pleasant crossing some of the streams in Arkansas which cut through the land. Some were easy to ford, others cost many weary miles of detour; often the banks were too steep and dangerous for the cattle and the wagons. There were few towns on the trails, and after they left Fort St. Louis, they met few travelers.

On the Sabbath evenings they would pitch their tents with the view of remaining until Monday, and on Sunday all the ordinances of the church would be attended. They read the Scriptures, had preaching, singing, breaking of bread and receiving of members. Thus, the wilderness of the plains was made the temple of praise by this group of Christians. Through Missouri and Arkansas, they slowly made their way to Louisiana, stopping at Natchez, Natchatoches, and Logansport. It was here, at Logansport, that they rested and waited to cross the Sabine River. They followed the trail called the Coushatta Trace, which was a road made by the Coushatta Indians in their migrations and tradings. They crossed the Sabine at Gaines Ferry and went west to the Angelina River. They crossed the Neches River below Fort Teran at Lewis's Ferry, and traveled across the Spanish Bluffs to Robbins' Ferry on the Trinity. They traveled slowly through this country, for there were no roads that crossed through the Coushatta Indian territory southwest to the town of Navasota.

The first permanent settlements in this country were made by members of Stephen F. Austin's colony. Jared E. Groce had built a stage stop in 1833. The first post office in this area was located at Fanthorp's Inn, in 1835. Jared Groce had planted cotton in this country, and had established the first gin in Texas at the site in 1828. Thus, when the Parker family moved into the southwestern part of Grimes County, they found a post office, a gin, and a stage stop. Here they camped and stayed about a year and a half. Another baby was born to Silas and Lucy, making the family of four children complete. There were now Cynthia Ann and John, who were the oldest, and Silas Jr. and the baby girl. After this rest, they loaded their wagons and put their faithful oxens to the carts and turned their faces to the northwest. The women and children remained at Grimes Prairie, in the summer of 1834, while James and Silas Parker and Elisha Anglin visited this northern country in Limestone County, which was then called Robertson's colony. There, they located their claims. Anglin placed a claim where the present town of Groesbeck is located. Silas Parker staked a claim north of Anglin's, and James Parker still further north. Then they returned to Grimes Prairie with their good news.

The caravan of the Parkers came up the east side of the Navasota river until they struck the old San Antonio Road.

This road was made by the Spanish traveling from San Antonio to Nacogdoches. They crossed over the river to the west bank and camped. There wasn't any road through that wilderness, just a kind of trail made by buffalo hunters who came to the prairie for their meat. The group passed through Boon Prairie, which is in Robertson county, to Duck Creek along old Euta, which was east of the frontier village of Kosse. They left the timbered country near a place called Spillers Point. Governor Brown later made this his ranch home, and named it Gentry Point.

A hunting party had come out to the prairie to kill buffalo; one of the men was named Spillers. The Indians got after them and killed Spillers, years before, and so it was always called Spillers Point. The caravan was now out of the timber upon the prairie, which was a great and beautiful expanse that reached across Texas. The faithful oxen moved on. They crossed Stelle's Creek, at what is known as the Old Tidwell Place, but there is no settlement there now. They built some cabins here of post oak logs. They called this Brown's fort for one of Daniel Parker's sons-in-law; it was on San Pedro Creek in the present Houston County, near the north line of the present town of Grapeland.

From this place, the Parker clan scattered in several directions. Daniel Parker took his children and went a few miles north to the community that is now the city of Elkhart, in Anderson County, and there built their homes and church. Here he established the church he had organized in Illinois and called it his "Pilgrim Predestinarian Regular Baptist Church," in the year 1833. This first church was of logs, and the present church is of stone. Daniel Parker was at this time a man of fifty-two years, and later became famous as one of the signers of the Declaration of Independence for Texas in 1836. He preached to his people until his death in Anderson County in 1845. After the battles of Alamo and Goliad, he joined Sam Houston and fought in the battle of San Jacinto. Because of the lack of communication, poor roads and transportation, the welfare of the rest of his brothers who had gone further west was slow in coming to his ears. His grave is now by the side of the church, and the cemetery back of the old building is full of the graves of his descendants.

Silas, James, and Benjamin, with their old father, Elder John, were more adventurous and pushed on to the west. They first took their families to the last fort which was felt to be safe from Indian attack. This was Fort Houston, about two miles west of the present city of Palestine, in Anderson County on the Trinity River. They arrived there in the spring of 1835. A store and half a dozen cabins were built around the fortifications, constituted as the first Texas town to bear the name of Sam Houston. The fort was an important point of frontier defense from 1836-1839. It was abandoned in 1841, but there is a marker erected at the fort today, placed by the Texas Centennial Commission. Miss Kate Hunter took the lead in securing a stone gateway and markers for the pioneer graves in Ft. Houston cemetery.

This country was full of flowing streams, verdant timber, and rich fertile soil, and promised a good livelihood to the sturdy pioneers. Young Silas Parker and Lucy were eager to push on and build a cabin of their own, for they had caught this westward fever from their father and felt the alluring call of this life of pioneering. They crossed the Trinity River and went west forty-five miles to the head of the Navasota River in the present Limestone County, near the place where the town of Groesbeck stands today. In the spring of 1834, the two brothers erected Parker's Fort, a kind of wooden barricade or wall around their cabins as a means of protection against the hostile Indians. They now consisted of eight or nine families. Elder John was the leader who had inspired them to move this far west.

Thus, the trek from five states to the West had ended for Grandfather John Parker. He had started in Virginia, and had traveled from Virginia to Georgia, from Georgia to Tennessee, from Tennessee to Illinois, and from Illinois to Texas. He was now seventy-six years of age, and had moved over 3000 miles on foot and horseback in his one span of life. The unexplored West had beckoned him on, and as he moved West, his rifle had not hung on the mantle or his Bible gathered dust, but with his gun across his shoulders he went seeking a new country for his children and future generations. He had fortified his descendants with courage and faith, for he had received a promise as did Abraham of old. He had obeyed an inner voice pushing him on: "Get thee out of thy country, and from thy kindred and from thy father's house, unto a land that I will show thee, and I will make of thee a great nation and I will bless thee."

Life At Fort Parker

THE STURDY PIONEERS had one enemy that they must always prepare for, and that was the red man whose land they were confiscating. To protect their families, stock, and crops, they had to erect forts for protection. These were placed in strategic places as a defense against the Indian. They could defy nature by bringing along a few scientific aids, but against enraged Indians they had to have walls to protect them from poisoned arrows. When the rich, fertile lands around Fort Parker began to be tilled, they realized that the roaming Comanche would not be long in taking his revenge against the civilization they were trying to produce. His habitat was not too far to the northwest, for the Comanche roamed up the Trinity and Brazos rivers to the Red River that rose in the buffalo country of the great plains.

Fort Parker was not far different from any of the frontier forts. Many of the forts in the east were made of green logs and were just pilings standing upright some twenty feet high, sharpened on the ends. On the inside were comfortable, durable log-houses placed at strategic points. This was well, until the red man learned that green logs dry out, and dry logs will burn when set with a pine torch.

From the Trinity River to the Brazos was a distance of seventy-five miles. The location that James and Silas Parker chose was at the headwaters of the Navasota. It was forty-five miles west of Fort Houston, and thirty miles east from the falls of the Brazos. Pedro de Rivera in 1727 had called this river the Navasota, and it has retained this name. Silas and James Parker started their fort over a hundred years later, for it was in the year 1835 that it was completed. Parker's Fort had its block houses, cabins, and stockades. The entire enclosure was larger than many of the earlier forts, for they wanted several families to live within its walls. It was about 234 feet long and about 200 feet wide. The stockades were some ten or twelve feet high, snugly built with well-trimmed logs. Each log had been pointed at the top to prevent the Indians from climbing over the walls. These were placed closely together so that the Indian could not get his arrow in the openings, or try to set fire to the inside. It must have taken hours upon hours with the crude tools to build the wall around the homes. The blockhouses projected some three feet beyond the outer walls of the cabins and stockades. These were vantage points to fire from when the enemy came close to the walls. There were ladders inside of the blockhouses which the men used to get up into the lofts. Holes were made in the logs so that the men could find an opening for their guns to aim at the enemy. The entire wall enclosed more than one acre of ground. There were just two lookouts, one on the left and one on the right at opposite corners, so that they could command every side of the fort that might be attacked. The trees around the fort had been cut down and the land cleared some distance back, so that they could not be used by the Indians for a surprise attack.

One of the most important parts of the fort was the gate. There was an inner door and an outer gate. The gate was a large folding one, made of thick slabs facing the path down to the river. This made it easier for them to get their water supply. This outer gate was tightly closed in time of emergency, and all men sat at their portholes at proper heights and distances. It was most difficult to build one of these forts, since the wood was put together by the craftsman's notch. They did not have any nails or irons. There was a sort of vestibule or enclosure for added safety within the large closing gates. One small door led from here into the grounds of the inside fort. In case the Indians got in the one gate, there was still the protection of the inner door.

There was one door at the back of the fort near the blockhouse. This was kept open most of the time, since the fields which they were cultivating were to the south and accessible from that direction. The gate was bulletproof and, as the Indians had only their bows and arrows, afforded a great deal of protection. This refuge of safety seems very trifling today to those who have fought in modern warfare, but they answered the purpose of the hardy pioneers against their dangerous enemy the Indian. They felt secure when inside this enclosure and were happy with their new home and the few belongings they had brought so far.

Inside the acre of ground were the cabins. They were placed on two sides of the enclosure, four on one side to the south next to the barricades and three houses on the north wall next to the garden. The houses were the same size and looked identical, being built of split logs. Each house was about twenty feet by ten, and today would seem very small for a family with several children. They had a fireplace each and a stick and dirt chimney, for the winters were cold. The walls were rough inside, and against them was placed a bed crudely made out of boards. There was no rocking chair, no dresser, no stove. The bedstead was a fixture to the cabin. It was the old post bedstead crudely made out of board with one post and the other end attached to the cabin walls. Three-legged stools were used for chairs. A table was another necessary part of the furniture.

A few pots and pans were all that these people had. The cooking vessels consisted of skillets and a bread pan, usually not more than two pots, one large and one small. They had two or three straw mattresses and the old spinning wheel which they had brought with them from Illinois, used to spin the thread for their clothes. A candle mold hung on the wall, and an old-fashioned heavy iron was placed on a small shelf above the fireplace. The floors were not made of wood, but of earth, pressed down and hardened by the many feet that wore it down. Guns hung on the wall, for they were ever needed for protection against the Indians. The cabin was made without the use of a nail. The door was built of three-foot boards by boring a hole through the board and into the upright with a gimlet, and pegging the boards on with wooden pegs; the door was hung on wooden hinges.

One of the greatest problems was to get corn. They traded cattle for corn at the Old San Antonio crossing down on the Navasota River. The hardest items to keep were bread and salt. They had plenty of meat, deer, and buffalo. All they had to do was take the rifle and go out and get it. But the meal was made to go a long way, for the nearest mill was 125 miles down the river.

They were fortunate in having plenty of water and wood. To the north a few miles was Tiwockena springs, which the Indians had named and used to get water for their horses and cattle. The farms which the men had adjoined the fort, and there was much timber in the region, with abundant rock which could be used for building, and salt licks, since game was plentiful. These rolling hills were covered with bountiful grazing for their stock. Water was plentiful in every creek. Game and fish were easily within reach. The medium-sized pine and pinoak were easily used for building their houses. The slender ash, gum, and blackjack were handy for corrals, and pole fences were made from them to hold stock.

It took brawn as well as brains to pick and properly notch the logs of these one-room dwellings. Split shingles were made of gum and ash, the cracks chinked with a bluish clay found in the creek banks. The windows were small openings in the day, but usually closed at night. Every pioneer community had a smokehouse where they hung and dried the beef, venison, and pork. This was some distance outside of the fort. The clearing of the land was most difficult indeed. There were no stump pullers, dynamite, or bulldozers to remove the stubborn oaks. The fields outside the fort consisted of only a few acres at first, then yearly, as they cleared and burned back a few more feet, they increased their productive activity. Life was real, but life was fragrant in this newly born Eden. There was the smell of dogwood blooms and redbuds, and wild flowers filled the rain-scented air of an early morning.

They planted a garden inside the fort, in which they raised corn, beans, peas, etc., as well as the larger plots of ground outside. The call of the bluejay, the warning of the robin, the music of the mocking bird, could all be heard throughout the day. The little creeks were jumping with the trout, the perch, and the channel cat. Life was rugged, full of toils and pains, but refreshing and invigorating in the early days of the building of Ft. Parker.

Children were taught to watch the weeds for the copperhead snake, the bush for the wild animals, and the trail for the lurking Comanche. These sturdy pioneers had pushed within the danger zone when they left Ft. Houston, which was forty-five miles away, with the Trinity River lying between them and safety. Their cap-and-ball rifle, plus a cap-and-ball six-shooter now and then, made up their defensive weapons. They had to mold their bullets, keep their powder dry, and take especial care of the barrels of their guns. They ground their corn as best they could, and meal and wheat for their bran flour when they could not go 125 miles to the nearest gristmill. They usually killed their hogs and beef in a community place, where the copper kettles were kept, scaffolds on which to hang meat; and they met together for their hog-killing day. They rendered their hog-lard together, as they did most of the frontier tasks in the community. There was brotherhood, mutual helpfulness that consisted of log-rollings, quiltings, clearings and buildings erected for one another. Their progress as well as their existence depended on mutual co-operation. The sick never wanted for visitors, the poor never wanted for bread, for it was all for one and one for all.

They must help each other, for they were isolated in this area. The nearest help of any kind must come from Fort Houston, which is now two miles from the present city of Palestine. They usually kept their stock outside, but in case of any warning of danger, the horses and cattle were driven in the stockade, for the settlers knew that the Indians desired these horses and cattle more than anything else which they owned. Anything of value which they had was kept in the walls of the fort, and they were ready at a moment's notice to close the gates and protect themselves from the Indians.

The Fort Parker community, when settled in 1835, was composed of the following families. One cabin was occupied by Grandfather John Parker and his wife, whom they called "Granny." Three of the other cabins were occupied by his three sons, James, Silas, and Benjamin. James Parker had two married daughters, Mrs. Rachel Plummer and Mrs. Sarah Nixon, and they occupied two of the cabins with their husbands and children. James had two more unmarried

children. Silas now had four children, Cynthia Ann, John, and two others. In all, there were some twenty-two relatives of the Parker family. Mrs. Nixon's mother and her sister, Mrs. Elizabeth Kellogg, were in this group, as was Mrs. Duty. Since James and Silas married Martha and Lucy Duty, it is presumed that they were sisters, and that their mother, Mrs. Duty, was with them.

There were two families, unrelated to the Parkers, who came with the convoy and helped build the fort. One was Samuel M. Frost, his wife and two children, and G. E. Dwight, also with his wife and two children. In all, there were about thirty-four persons in and around the fort. There were some settlers within the distance of the fort who wanted the protection during times of danger, but did not desire to live within the stockade. They were an older man by the name of Lunn; Mr. David Faulkenberry and his son Evan; Silas Bates; and a boy, Abram Anglin. They had erected small log cabins and cleared their small farms, and were working on them in this season of the spring. All of these settlers had had a long journey from Illinois, and they were glad to find a place to call home. Cynthia Ann was eight years old when the fort was completed at last, and they made their home in Texas on the Navasota River.

CHAPTER III

Texas -- 1833-1836

DURING THESE FEW YEARS when the Parkers first arrived in Texas, the Texans and Mexicans lived at peace with one another, and there was little thought of revolution. But there were differences which caused trouble in the cultural and political traditions of these two people. The Americans like Silas Parker were the personification of individualism, while the Mexican had a reverence for authority. The American interpretation of self-government was hopelessly at odds with the central government of the people of Mexico.

Law of April 6, 1830. The Mexican government was to undertake large colonization programs aimed at settling large numbers of Mexicans in Texas, and no more immigrants from the United States were to be admitted. Soon the colonists found themselves surrounded by garrisons of soldiers, even as far north as Velasco, near the mouth of the Brazos and Nacogdoches. The Texans resented the presence of the soldiers.

Santa Anna. Santa Anna was meeting with great success in his revolution. On July 16, 1832, some of the soldiers at these garrisons declared for Santa Anna, and since he won his revolution, the Texans were free to conduct their government without military interference.

The Convention of 1832. As Santa Anna continued to win battles in the war against the Mexican government, the Texans felt that the time was ripe to ask for certain governmental reforms. A call was sent from San Felipe for a convention to meet in that city on October 1, 1832. Each settlement was to send five delegates. Stephen F. Austin was elected president of the convention, and F. W. Johnson, secretary. They adopted a number of resolutions requesting a complete tariff exemption, that the immigration law be modified so as to permit more immigration from the United States, and that a commissioner be appointed to issue land titles to the East Texas settlers; also that the Indian problem be attended to at once. However, the work of the convention came to naught. The Mexicans at San Antonio had refused to participate. The chief held the convention to be unauthorized and null.

The Convention of 1833. It was to this convention that Silas and James Parker went as representatives of the municipality of Vicesca. The convention worked for about two weeks, petitioning for the repeal of the anti-immigration law, for renewed tariff exemption, and for the erection of a State of Texas. Sam Houston, representing Nacogdoches, was chairman of the committee which wrote the constitution for the state. Three commissioners, Austin, Miller, and Erasmo Seguin of San Antonio, were chosen to present the petitions to the government. In the end, Austin went alone.

Austin in Mexico. Austin left San Felipe in April, 1833, to go to Mexico City. More than two years elapsed before he returned to the banks of the Brazos. The government of Mexico granted some reforms, for the anti-immigration article was repealed, and an investigation of the tariff exemption was promised. Austin left Mexico City on December 10, 1833. He had failed to obtain statehood for Texas, but had brought about certain important reforms. But Austin was arrested and sent to Mexico City on February 13, 1834. He was never charged before any court, but his case was declared to be within the scope of a general amnesty law and he was released on Christmas Day of 1834.

A Convention at San Felipe, October 16, 1835. Just as many wars begin, the Texas revolt against Santa Anna began at Gonzales, the Lexington of Texas. It was over a disputed cannon which had been given to the people of Gonzales for protection against the Indians. By refusing to give up the cannon, the Texans challenged Mexican military authority. A band of Texans captured Goliad and San Antonio, but the colonists knew that Santa Anna's legions would arrive in the spring.

The representatives of the Texans assembled at San Felipe on October 16, and James Parker and Silas Parker were elected delegates to meet in the convention. They represented the municipality of Vicesca. They were forced to adjourn, but on November 3, they had the required number of members present. The members were divided. One group stood for immediate declaration of independence, while another thought they should fight for the Mexican federal constitution which Santa Anna had overthrown.

The Declaration of November 7. This pledged the loyalty of the Texans to the constitution of 1824, and appealed to the Mexican liberals to join in the fight against the dictatorship of Santa Anna. This group then created a provisional or temporary government. They chose the members of the provisional government, and Sam Houston was appointed by the consultation, commissioned by the governor, subject to orders of the governor and council. Houston was to command only the regular army, which had yet to be created. Both Daniel and James Parker were at this conference, and Daniel Parker is one of those who signed the papers for the declaration.

The Declaration of Independence. The general convention was called, meeting at Washington on the Brazos on March 1, 1836. By this time, James Parker had returned to Fort Parker, but Daniel Parker had stayed to take a part in these proceedings. This was the adoption of a formal Declaration of Independence, in which the people of Texas openly declared themselves free of Mexican rule and appealed to relatives, friends, and sympathizers in the United States to aid them in the fighting. A constitution was drawn up and signed by the delegates. The convention not only had the duty of declaring independence and writing a constitution, but had to make provision for the conduct of the war, and create a government to serve until the constitution could be placed in operation. For commander-in-chief, they again turned to Sam Houston. They gave Houston command over all men in the field — volunteers, militia and the regular army. They created the "ad interim" government to serve until order could be restored, and the constitution adopted.

The Siege of the Alamo. Lack of leadership led to great confusion during January and February of 1836. Santa Anna was preparing an army of 6000 men to march against the Texans. Colonel William Travis had been sent to San Antonio with thirty men of the regular army. General Houston sent Colonel Bowie to San Antonio with instructions to demolish the fortification, and leave. The active command fell upon Travis, for Bowie became ill. Travis prepared to defend the Alamo with about 160 men. The exact number of Texans killed at the Alamo is not known. No Texas soldier remained alive. Several women and children were spared. The Texas people determined to avenge the deaths of Travis, Bowie, Crockett, Bonham, and all of those who had fought with them. The battle cry now came to be "Remember the Alamo."

The Goliad Campaign. James W. Fannin, who was in command at Goliad, is the most tragic figure of the Texas Revolution. He lacked the ability to make decisions in a reasonable time, and he is regarded as having been careless. When the Mexican army approached San Antonio, Travis had called on Fannin for aid. He did not have a sufficient number of wagons and oxen to transport all his artillery and supplies, and so returned to Goliad. Houston had ordered Fannin to retreat to Victoria. Fannin was in no hurry, and permitted the Mexicans to surround him at the battle of the Coleto. The cause of the Texans was hopeless, and they raised a white flag. On March 26, Portilla received orders from Santa Anna to execute immediately all prisoners who had been captured in battle. On the following morning, the prisoners were divided into three groups, marched out to the prairie, and shot. Santa Anna bears the responsibility for the massacre of these 300 men.

The Battle of San Jacinto Campaign. The victories of the Mexicans at Goliad and San Antonio made them confident. The destiny or the fate of Texas lay in the little force at Gonzales and the few volunteers that could be obtained under the leadership of General Houston. It is now that Daniel Parker, fifty-two years of age, came to the general, and offered his services as a volunteer. Houston took command at Gonzales on March 11, and, learning of the fall of the Alamo, retreated to the Colorado. The army reached the Brazos at San Felipe, and after suffering the loss of two companies, moved up the river to the Groce plantation near the present city of Hempstead. Santa Anna reached San Felipe on April 7.

The Texans left Groce's April 14, having received two

six-pound cannons given to them by the people of Cincinnati. On April 19, Houston told the soldiers they would have their opportunity of fighting and avenging the disasters of Goliad and the Alamo. The Texans moved down Buffalo Bayou, and on April 20 reached the San Jacinto River. In front of them, for perhaps two miles, stretched a prairie. The Mexicans established themselves on the southern edge of the prairie, with the marshes to their backs.

It was on April 21, 1836, that about 800 men faced a force of men, under Santa Anna, estimated at 1200. They attacked the Mexicans at three o'clock in the afternoon. Taken by surprise, the Mexicans fled in terror before the fighting Texans. The actual fighting lasted only eighteen minutes, with about 630 Mexicans killed in battle, while the Texan loss was only two killed and twenty-three wounded. Santa Anna managed to escape, but was captured the following day. This victory was of great importance to the Texans, but the capture of Santa Anna made it doubly so. With Santa Anna as a prisoner, the Mexican forces were unable to continue the war. The Texans had advanced to within 200 yards of the enemy camp without being noticed. This battle is the most important battle in the history of Texas. It won for Texas the independence which had been declared at Washington weeks before, and launched the Republic of Texas upon its future for ten years. It made secure the lives and property of the settlers who had come, like the Parkers, to Texas. It encouraged more immigration from the United States, and the country was opened to rapid settlement by the aggressive Americans.

Santa Anna was forced to issue orders to his commanders to retreat to the western part of the state and stop all military activity. There were two treaties made, one secret and one public. The public treaty provided that war was to cease, that Santa Anna would not take up arms against the

Texans, and that the Mexican soldiers were to leave as soon as possible. By the secret agreement, Santa Anna was to use his influence in Mexico in obtaining the recognition of Texas independence, providing that the boundary of Texas should not extend beyond the Rio Grande. In return for signing these treaties, Santa Anna was to be sent to Vera Cruz. But the Mexican government did not accept either of these treaties. But the 4000 survivors of the army of Santa Anna crossed the Rio Grande and left their commander and several hundred of their men as prisoners of the Texans. The independence of Texas was never recognized by Mexico, but year by year, as her population increased, there was less reason to fear these enemies.

But while the Mexicans were threatening, the Indians were attacking the colonists in the year of 1835. So the new government of Texas took action and created the Texas Ranger. Silas Parker, father of Cynthia Ann, was the first regularly appointed Texas Ranger or military commander to serve on the staff in this manner. He had the distinction of being the first Texas Ranger appointed in the North Texas area. Silas Parker's appointment is contained in the action of the General Council according to the report in the *Telegraph and Texas Register,* printed at San Felipe on October 26, 1835. He was to secure the inhabitants residing on the frontier from the invasion of hostile Indians. The General Council had made arrangements for raising three companies of Rangers. There were to be twenty-five men, under Silas M. Parker, to range between the Brazos and the Trinity, both companies to be stationed at the Waco village, which was about forty miles west of Fort Parker. There were to be ten men under Garrison and Green, to be stationed at Fort Houston, to protect the country east of the Trinity.

When the families at Fort Parker learned of the defeat of the Texans at the battles of the Alamo and Goliad, they put a few belongings in their carts, and fled before the invading army of Mexico. They reached the Trinity River, forty-five miles distant, only to find that they had to stop because of the overflow of the stream at that time of the year. But soon they heard the news that Santa Anna had been defeated at the Battle of San Jacinto, and that Texas was free from the Mexicans. They received this news joyfully and decided on a return to Fort Parker. Silas Parker and James took their families across the Trinity to Fort Houston, since they were so near, and got supplies which they put on horseback. This was in April of 1836. They had left their stock, and were anxious to get back in time to plant a crop for that season. It was about the 25th of April when they made their way back to Fort Parker. Little did they dream that, in roughly twenty-one days, many of that group would be killed by the Indians, and that Cynthia Ann and John would be captives of the Comanches.

CHAPTER IV

The Massacre

THE PARKER MEN, with the women and children, returned to Fort Parker to resume a normal life about April 25, 1836, rejoicing at the defeat of Santa Anna. The threat of danger from Indians seemed less, as their minds were filled with the news of the war for the independence of Texas. Silas Parker, Lucy, and their four children were very busy these days. Cynthia Ann was nine years old, and was able to help her mother with the sewing, and cooking, and tending of the other children. John, her brother, was six now, and tried to help his father around the garden. The two other children were a boy and a girl. The boy's name was Silas, for his father, but the little girl's name is not known. They were a happy family, and there was much to be done in the home and in the field.

On the evening of May 18, 1836, the men had come in tired from their day's work in the adjoining fields; Silas had washed and they had eaten their home-cooked bread and meat outdoors, for the weather was warm for that time of year. Just a few days before, the troop of Rangers, which had been there for their protection, had been disbanded.

James and Silas Parker knew that these men wished to return to their homes, and since the Indian danger seemed less, the men had dispersed and left the fort unprotected. The danger from the Mexicans was past, but they failed to take into account the Indians who were watching until the troops left before launching an attack on the settlement.

On the morning of May 19, 1836, some of the men who had fields about a mile from the fort left to work them. These were Uncle James, and two men, Nixon and Plummer. For some reason, Silas did not go to the field that morning. Grandfather John, and Granny, Silas Parker and his wife Lucy, Cynthia Ann and John, and the two other smaller chilrdren, were all busy within the stockade with their daily tasks. There were other women and children also in the fort as well as Benjamin Parker. Silas and Robert Frost had not left, but were working on their part of the garden inside the fort.

It was about nine o'clock when the cry of Indians was heard in the distance; and as the alarm was given, they looked and saw several hundred Comanche and Kiowa Indians approaching within yards of the fort. In the excitement, the gate had not been shut as it should have been that morning. But as the Indians presented a white flag and made the signs of friendship, the few men in the fort were not alarmed. There were only six men in the fort, and about ten women and fifteen children. The Indians told Benjamin Parker, who went out to meet them, that they were looking for a camping place, and inquired about the location of water. They asked for beef, for they said they were very hungry and in need of food. Benjamin returned to the fort and told his brother Silas that he was fearful of these Indians, that they were hostile, but that he would go again and talk with them.

Cynthia Ann's father, Silas, begged him not to go, but

Benjamin would not listen. He was immediately surrounded and killed. At the sight of blood, the savages began their wild, yelling cries. One can imagine the fear in the hearts of those women and children inside the gates. The Indians then charged upon the fort. Silas Parker fell on the outside of the fort as he was trying to save the life of his niece, Mrs. Rachel Plummer. There was no one with the presence of mind to close the stockade doors, which would have at least given them a chance for survival. Rachel Plummer made a terrible struggle, but was knocked down with a hoe and taken captive. Samuel F. Frost and his son Robert were killed inside, while defending the women and children left in the stockade.

At the beginning of the trouble, some of the women ran for help through the small back door of the stockade. The Indians seemed to pour into the fort; there was no stopping them. Elder John Parker, his wife, and Mrs. Kellogg attempted to escape through the back door and had gone about three-fourths of a mile from the fort when they were overtaken and driven back. Here Grandfather John Parker, seventy-nine years of age, was murdered, scalped, and mutilated. He had come from Virginia — to end his life here on the prairies of Texas at the hands of hostile Indians. His wife was speared and left for dead. Mrs. Kellogg was taken captive. The four men who were in the fort that morning had been killed

When the Indians had first cried out and come to the fort that morning, Cousin Sarah Nixon had escaped also through the back door to tell Uncle James, her husband, and Mr. Plummer, of the attack. She reached them distraught and breathless, as she ran to warn them. Mr. Plummer hurried on to tell the Faulkenberrys, Lunn, Bates and the Anglins, who lived in nearby cabins. James Parker and Nixon started on to the fort to see if they could save anyone.

James was met soon by his wife and children, who had also run from the Indians, so he took them some five miles down the Navasota River, and secreted them in the bottoms of the river for safety.

Although Nixon did not have any arms, he continued on to the fort and met Cynthia Ann's mother with her four children. The Indians forced the mother to lift Cynthia Ann and John behind two of the Comanches who were on horses. Sobbing, the two frightened children were taken away, while the Indians on foot took the mother and the two smaller children with Nixon back to the fort.

Just as the Indians were about to kill Nixon, David Faulkenberry, who had been warned by Mr. Plummer, appeared with his rifle and caused them to fall back. Nixon, after his narrow escape from death, was very much excited and left to search for his wife. He found Sarah Nixon and their children with Dwight and the Frost family, and soon overtook James Parker and went with him to the hiding place on the river bottom.

Faulkenberry was now left with Mrs. Parker, Cynthia Ann's mother, and the two small children. With one in her arm and leading the other, they tried to get away from the fort. The Indians who followed them were held in check by the brave man's rifle. Several warriors on horses charged at them, but they retreated as Faulkenberry aimed his gun at them. They continued until they passed through a prairie of some forty or fifty acres. Just as they entered the woods, one Indian made a desperate charge, and Mrs. Parker's faithful dog seized the horse by the nose, causing the rider and horse to fall. It was at this crucial moment that Silas Bates, Abram Anglin, and Evan Faulkenberry came up, causing the Indians to retire. Thus the mother of Cynthia Ann and the two small children were saved from the massacre.

But Mrs. Parker had lost her husband and her two children; Cynthia Ann, who was nine years old, and John, who was six, were taken captive by the Indians. Her heart was grieved over the loss of her beloved husband and the terrible ordeal of suffering she felt awaited her children at the hands of the Indians. She was never to see them again, and never knew their fate. Mrs. Parker and the children, with these men, secreted themselves in a small creek bottom, not too far from the family of James Parker, who had also hidden in this river bottom. Each was unconscious of the other being close by, but because of the danger they dared not move or make any sound, for they were fearful of their lives. They spent the night of May 19 in the open woods, cold, and hungry, and spent with grief over the death of their loved ones and the capture of their children.

As soon as nightfall came, two of the men, Anglin and Evan Faulkenberry, started back to the fort to see if they could help any of the wounded or find any who might have escaped. They passed by Faulkenberry's cabin, and here they saw a strange sight. They thought it was a ghost, but it was Granny Parker. Anglin says that he was scared worse by this white ghost than when the attack was at its height. The men hesitated, and the ghost beckoned them to come to her. It was indeed old Granny Parker. The Indians had wounded and stripped and left her for dead. She had made her way to the house from the fort by crawling the entire distance. The men took some bedclothing from the house, and carried her for a distance, and made a bed, covering her and making her as comfortable as they could. They told her they would come back after they returned from the fort. She told them that she had left some silver hidden under a hickory bush, and asked them to bring it back with them.

The scene, on arriving at the fort, was most terrible. There was no one alive, but the dogs were barking, the cattle lowing, the horses neighing, and the hogs squealing, as if panicked by the presence of death. Taking the silver, $106.50, but finding no one else alive, they returned to where they had hidden Granny Parker. Tenderly they carried her back to the bottoms, where they had left the other women and children. Nixon returned to the bottoms, and Plummer was not seen for six days. As though aroused from a dream, he started out, with only a butcher knife, to hunt his wife and children, and was seen no more for six days. The shock of the attack was almost more than they could survive.

There seemed to be no sign of the Indians, who had gone with their captives. They had taken Mrs. Rachel Plummer (daughter of James W. Parker), and her son James Pratt Plummer, who was just two years old, Mrs. Elizabeth Kellogg, Cynthia Ann, and her brother John. They had killed Grandfather John Parker and Silas Parker, the grandfather, and father of Cynthia Ann. Her uncle, Benjamin F. Parker, and two of their friends, Samuel M., and his son Robert Frost, were also dead. They had wounded old Granny Parker and Mrs. Duty, but these had escaped capture.

On the next morning, Bates, Anglin, and Evan Faulkenberry went back to the fort to get provisions for those who escaped and to secure horses to ride, as well as to bury the dead. They found five or six horses, a few saddles and some meal, bacon, and honey. They were still afraid that the Indians were close by, so they left without burying the dead men and women. They returned to the weeping women and children in the bottom of the creek, and waited there all that day, not starting through the woods until that night of the 19th. They went east toward Fort Houston, which was the nearest place where they could get help. It took them six days and nights to travel the forty-five miles from Fort Parker to Ft. Houston.

They wandered on suffering for want of food, their clothing torn by the bushes and thorns and trees. Their feet were bleeding, especially those of the women and children, for they had no shoes. They finally reached Tinnin's at the old San Antonio and Nacogdoches crossing of the Navasota. Two men met them there, a Mr. Carter and Mr. Courtney, with five horses. Then some of the women and children could ride. The people around there had just returned to their deserted homes after the victory of San Jacinto, but they shared all they had of clothing and food. Then they moved on to Fort Houston. In a short time, the families located temporarily as best suited each family, but most of them returned to Fort Parker not long afterwards.

A burial party went back from Ft. Houston, consisting of twelve men. The remains now lie near the site of old Fort Parker. The only slab of marble is the grave of Elder John Parker, which is in the center of the fort, now restored. The other graves are unmarked, with not even a slab to tell of their battle with life and with the savages who killed them. The Indians left immediately with their booty, traveling among the hills and valleys of the rivers to the west. On hearing of the tragedy, Major John W. Moody was ordered with 500 troops to avenge the massacre and find the Indians, but just as they prepared to go after these Indians, word came that Santa Anna was returning to Texas to fight, and they were ordered to meet this invading force. James Parker was one who returned to bury his father and brother Silas. His own immediate family had all been saved, except for his daughter Rachel and her small two-year-old boy. He took his family back to the fort on June 19, but they found the crops destroyed, the horses stolen, the cattle killed, and all the furniture gone.

These are the known facts of the capture of Cynthia Ann, who was taken from her loving mother by the Indians.

She was snatched from the comparative civilization of the pioneer home to the wild Indians' ways when she was nine years of age. It is known that she had blond hair and blue eyes, and that she was tall and sturdily built. The last time she saw her mother was when she looked back from the Indian horse as she was riding away, not knowing her fate or that of her mother. Fear filled her heart and mind, as she realized that she would probably never see her loved ones again.

CHAPTER V

A Captive

THE COMANCHE BRAVE, when on the warpath, experiences a savage intoxication of lust to kill and plunder. It usually lasts for a few hours, during which period of insensibility only a superior power can check him in his depredation. After the intoxication for blood is over, his mind turns to a coonish inquisitiveness to inspect the things to which he has access.

The massacre being over, they entertained themselves by searching every crack and cranny for objects of booty. Old trunks, treasure chests, and medicine cabinets were alluring objects for their canny eyes.

Having plundered everything in the fort, they cut open the bed ticks of the feather mattresses, scattering them like dust in the air with the hopes of finding something that the white man had hidden. Strange as it may seem, they attached some value to books, and would gather them up and take them along with them. They could not read, but there was something about the bound volumes that caught their curiosity. Garden tools, axes, or any other iron objects were considered useful in making an effective weapon. Naturally they searched every corner for rifles, powder, and bullets.

Everything which they did not want, they tore up or destroyed with childish and fiendish glee.

The captives whom they had killed, they scalped at once. The Indian preferred that his victim not be dead. The work could be more gracefully done, they thought, while the blood flowed freely. The flow of rich, warm, human blood was a balm to the savage nature. The scalp slipped more easily when warm, and satisfied the urge to inflict suffering. Their custom was to place the moccasined feet firmly on the neck of the prostrate victim, catch the hair of the head tightly in the left hand, and, with a sharp knife in the right hand, cut entirely around the head near the hairline, cutting through the cuticle to the skull; then, with strong pressure of the foot and with both hands firmly gripping the hair, giving a quick, hard jerk. The scalp slipped clean and, with a dull thud, left the entire skull exposed. The possessor, in great delight, took the scalp as a much treasured trophy, and with pride had it attached to his belt at the next war dance.

When the coonish curiosity was over, and they had looked and searched every part of the fort on the inside, they began to think about the results of their depredation. It was not far to Fort Houston, and they realized that help for the white people could be on its way soon. They did not know how many of the settlers had escaped, but they knew they would surely warn the neighboring frontiersman about their successful raid. The Comanche, when drunk on human blood, was a brave, dangerous man; when his combative ardor cooled, he would not resist very strongly. But when the excitement of battle was over, he preferred flight to facing the enemy.

The Indians rounded up their captives like cattle and started in a northwesterly direction toward their Comanche territory that extended to the Red River. The captives, by this time, were almost senseless from the shock. It seems they left the fort in small bands, except those with the Comanches and the Kiowas, who traveled together. It was a fast, hard march until midnight to get as far away as possible from the white man's rifle. The Indians halted on an open prairie, hobbled their horses, placed their guards, and began to arrange their camp. The hour to assemble their booty and to celebrate had come.

They brought their prisoners together for the first time. Their hands were tied behind them with rawhide thongs, tied so tightly that they cut the flesh. Their feet were bound together, and they were laid upon their faces. The Indians formed a semicircle around them and got ready for their dance of victory. There were five captives, two women and three children. The two women were Mrs. Rachel Plummer, the daughter of James Parker, Cynthia Ann's own cousin, and Mrs. Elizabeth Kellogg, a relative by marriage. They had captured Mrs. Plummer's small boy, who was two years old; Cynthia Ann, who was nine at this time; and her brother John, who was six years of age. They had brought along with them several of the bloody scalps, which the poor captives well recognized as being those of their grandfather and their own father. They knew that some had escaped, but young Cynthia Ann, looking at this scene, did not know whether the rest of the community had been destroyed or not. It must have been a harrowing experience for young Cynthia Ann when the Comanche braves, smeared with war paint, commenced their war dance. They danced, screamed and yelled, slapping, cuffing, and beating their prisoners. Often the cry of a child could be heard above their insatiable screams, but they were soon hushed by blows until it seemed that none could survive. They were so dazed as to be, in a sense, immune to the horrors of that hour. In later years, it was shown that Cynthia Ann Parker remembered very little of that terrible ordeal.

The next morning the Indians pushed on, and it was not until the third night out, having gone more than 100 miles, that they now felt secure from their pursuers. It is believed that they camped where Weatherford now stands, and held another war dance around the campfires, and displayed the scalps of their victims in great rejoicing. The exact location of their campsite cannot be definitely determined. It may have been at Soldier's Spring, the old Chautauqua grounds, where Robert E. Lee and his men camped many years later, but more probably it was on the spring branch below Holland's Lake on Fred Cotten's land, where there is evidence of an old campsite.

The events of these days are known, for after Mrs. Rachel Plummer was saved and bought back by the white people, she wrote the narrative of her experiences with the Indians. They were now in the hands of a ruthless and savage enemy. They beat and whipped their captives, covering their flesh with bruises and wounds. The Indians had taken a bottle of pulverized arsenic from the white men's medicine cabinets. They had mistaken this for a kind of white war paint, and with this they painted their faces and bodies all over, after dissolving it with their saliva. Four of the Indians thus painted, died.

They went in a northerly direction, and the captives were tied every night for five nights. During the first five days, they did not give the prisoners any food, and only a scanty allowance of water. After they had reached the Grand Prairie, the prisoners were divided. Mrs. Elizabeth Kellogg was claimed by the Kitchawas. Six months after her capture, she was purchased by the Delaware Indians and returned to Nacogdoches, where she was delivered to General Houston at the price of $150.00. Mrs. Rachel Plummer was taken by another tribe that moved southeast toward the Rio

Grande. She remained captive for eighteen months. She gave birth to a child during her captivity. The Indians were very cruel to her, and she endured terrible suffering, for the child, a little boy, was tortured and killed before her eyes because of his crying. She was made a servant to the Indian family into which she was sent, and wandered over a great part of the West. Her husband never ceased, during this time, to look for her and the boy James, who was taken when he was only two years old and separated from his mother's arms. She was finally rescued, as her own story tells, by an American merchant, Mr. William Donahue, through a Mexican Agency in Sante Fe, New Mexico. It took seventeen long days to get to Sante Fe from the place where she was being held by the Indians. Then they took her to Independence, Missouri. There, her brother-in-law, L. D. Nixon, met her and took her back to her people in Texas. It was on Feb. 19, 1838, that she reached the home of her father, James Parker. She wrote of her experiences with the Indians, and they were published with a book by her father, James Parker. But so cruel had been the hardships, that she died just one year after reaching home on Feb. 19, 1839. She did not know at that time where her little boy, James, was, for he was not rescued from the Indians until after her death.

James Pratt Plummer was two when he was captured by the Indians, and after six long years the efforts of his grandfather, James Parker, were rewarded, and he was located and brought back to the white family. The tribe he had been given to was constantly on the move and traveled over much territory. He was at last ransomed and taken to Fort Gibson in February of 1843. James Parker went at once to find the boy, and identified him by his looks as the child of Rachel and brought him home. The boy James, now eight years old, had no recollection of his mother or of his home with the white people. The boy lived and became a citizen of Anderson County.

John Parker was given to one band of Comanches, and Cynthia Ann was given to the roving group that lived in the northwestern part of Texas, having very little contact with white people. There are two conflicting stories told about John Parker.

One is that he grew up among the Comanches and, when of age, fell in love with a Mexican girl who was a captive of the Indians. Before they arrived back from one of their raids, John took smallpox, and the Indian fear of this disease was so great they left him alone in this condition. The Mexican girl stayed with him and cared for him. They settled on a stock ranch in the far West, and John Parker joined a Mexican company in the Confederate service during the Civil War. He was not willing to leave Texas to fight, and returned home to live on his ranch across the Rio Grande. Then there is another story which discredits these findings.

Having traveled so much in Texas and Mexico, it is said that he became a professional guide. He is said to have joined the Confederate army, but when ordered to cross the Texas line, he returned to the Rio Grande Valley. On the way back, he stopped one night in Anderson County to visit an uncle whom he had not seen since his capture at Fort Parker when he was six years old. John was a peculiar fellow. There was not one drop of Indian blood which flowed through his veins, yet he looked like a typical Indian, with feathers decorating his hat. He talked very little and did not visit his relatives, not even his own sister, Cynthia Ann, who was not far away. He departed for the West, and no trace of him or his family has since been found.

It is known that the Texas legislature, in 1845, appropriated $300 for the finding of John Parker, but it was never used since Parker was not located until he was grown, and he would not then return to Texas. Many of these stories may be fiction, but it is known that he was six when he was captured in 1836. In some of the stories concerning Quanah Parker, who was Cynthia Ann's son, there is mention of a visit that Quanah made to the home of his uncle, John Parker, in Mexico, but if this is true it cannot be proven by written evidence.

Cynthia Ann, separated from her brother, gradually forgot the language of her people. As the years dragged on, she embraced the language, manners and customs of the Comanche. It is difficult to imagine how long the dazed mind of young Cynthia Ann retained the impressions of loved ones at the Fort, their home, and other American characteristics and ways. It would seem that the fear and tragedy of the massacre would have stamped an indelible impression upon her tender brain. But the mind is like a twig. It is often molded by present circumstances to a bent that is foreign and native. Cynthia Ann was torn from her flesh and blood at Fort Parker and separated from her brother at Grand Prairie, and it was many years before any tidings came of her whereabouts. Many efforts had been made through Indian scouts, and otherwise by traders, to locate her, but it seemed futile, for many years passed by without hearing any word of her welfare.

She was given to one of the families of the Comanche tribe, who gave her the Indian name "Preloch."

CHAPTER VI

Comanche Culture

THE LIFE of a quiet home surrounded by a godly atmosphere is a contrast indeed to the existence of a roving band of Comanches. The life at the fort had everything that bespeaks the best of a frontier culture and civilization. Cynthia Ann's home was graced with Christian parents, the reading of the Bible, and the best of care and home-cooked meals. This girl was taken from the loving care of a tender mother and suddenly thrust into the home of a life-hardened squaw who naturally had no love for a white-skinned girl. The sudden change of culture and habits was enough to wreck the mind and personality. Why the Comanche squaw spared her is inconceivable, unless she was forced to do so by an Indian brave.

This roving band of Comanches never spent over three or four days in one location. Whether this was nomadic fever, or a thinning out of game, is difficult to tell. Some have suggested that this was the Indians' mode of sanitation, but it was likely a case of a nomadic desire to see something farther up the river. In case of cold weather or storms, many times they remained longer in one place.

Cynthia Ann's nomadic life started at Fort Parker north-westward to the great plains of Texas.

Their homes were made of buffalo skins, in the main, stretched on poles. These were easily dismantled, the skins placed on the mule's back, and the poles swung across with a rawhide lariat. Their beds were the solid earth, plus a buffalo skin, and for cover sometimes a blanket. The Comanche braves seemed to give the women the distinct honor of doing all of the servile labor. They erected the teepees, herded the horses, loaded the pack-mules, dressed the skins, and cooked the meat. The brave was a lusty type of fellow who liked a good shade at noonday in which to snooze. Like the owl, he came out at night for his activities. The men danced every night and practiced their fierce orgies of war. In the meantime, the women were very attendant with their water, or such necessities as the games called for.

The councils were carried on entirely by the men. The squaws were never allowed to sit in council with the braves. They were not supposed to know anything, and were little more than servants, being treated accordingly. The art of cooking among the Comanches is not far different from that practiced by the other tribes. Their meat was broiled or sizzled over an open fire. The white man got his idea of open pit barbecue from the Indians. A few of the tribes boiled their meat. They parched their corn on a self-styled sandstone rock. The Comanches were very fond of hard parched corn and brown broiled venison. In season, they ate the wild fruits that the scanty country provided. The apple of the prickly pear became wholesome food. They were very fond of fowls, but it was so difficult to feed a band on these, so they did not spend much time shooting them. The buffalo, antelope, and deer, as well as the steer, comprised their chief means of sustenance.

They were plagued with a number of superstitions about

their cooking and eating. They would not broil and boil meat on the same fire. It was a sure sign of defeat and evil when these two were mixed over the same flame. They were sticklers for eating one food alone without admixture. Their superstition did not allow any person to pass near where meat was broiling or boiling; not even his shadow was supposed to fall across this food. This seems to give some reason why, in later years, they turned to dried meat as well as raw. When the buffalo was killed, they suffered very little of him to be lost. They did not believe in waste and extravagance in the killing of wild game. When a buffalo, elk, or deer was killed, the hunter and his family would gather about, open its veins, and drink the warm blood. Raw brains and the marrow from the leg bones, when stirred together, made an appetizing sauce upon the slaughtered animal's ribs. The fresh, warm liver, covered with bile of the gall bladder, was considered a first-rate delicacy. Liver cooked on coals, with the spread of brain and marrow on it, was a choice children's dish. Entrails stripped of their contents by pressing them between two fingers were often eaten raw and unwashed while still warm. The Comanche would cut into the udder of the female buffalo, place his mouth in the gash, and suck the warm mixture of milk and blood with the greatest of pleasure. The curdled milk from the stomach of a suckling fawn was thought to be rich fare indeed. These dishes are repulsive to the reader, but it provided an effective way of getting vitamins and iron in large quantities. It must be remembered that they raised no vegetables of their own, and their diet must provide them with strength and heat to endure the hardships of a life of exposure.

Little Cynthia Ann, taken from the warm comforts of a nice log cabin, enjoying the warm corn pone or yeast rolls for her breakfast, plus honey and butter with clean appetizing milk, was suddenly thrust and subjected to the above-mentioned barbaric ways of life. The sudden revolution of culture in a tender nine-year-old girl must have been of a nature that is beyond present imagination. Evidently she was born strong in body and mind, and inherited a graduate portion of common sense from her good frontier parents, for she must now adapt herself to the ways of the Comanches. For twenty-five long years of association with this culture overbalanced the nine years of her precious home care. Her personality was Indianized and she came to love and admire the hardihood of the Comanche life during this interval.

Cynthia Ann had been accustomed to worship on Sunday and a formal church service. There was worship in the Comanche's heart, for he said that no man is without his god. The Indians had a deep reverent spirit of worship in their savage hearts. They believed in the Great Spirit as a supernatural being of some nature. They had an intense feeling that they were being watched by this Great Spirit, to whom they were subject. There were times when the Great Spirit would become angry toward the Indian, and this anger would manifest itself in some calamity. It might be in a storm, a drought, or in the form of a ferocious animal, but he felt of a necessity that some form of worship must be given to his god.

Chief among these forms of worship was dancing. The Comanche also felt that torturing his prisoners was pleasing to his god. On the plains, the Comanche often paid homage to a large lump of platinum. This is a scarce and valuable metal that is known to be heavier and more durable than gold. Often arrows and spikes were made from this precious metal. This was found among the Indians, in lumps of considerable weight. In the cross timbers of the Brazos, much of this platinum was found. They had their yearly sacrifices, and their chiefs collected and prepared them for these services. The offerings usually consisted of beautiful beads, muscle shells, and periwinkles. They left these beads by the bushel, at the altar of their sacrifices. While traveling on the plains, it is found that they worshipped many things; one might worship a pet crow, another a deerskin with a picture of the moon on it; some groups might worship the eagle; but all of these objects were kept sacred. In all of this strange array, there is found the belief in a supreme being, the resurrection of the body, and future rewards and punishments. They buried the brave with his bows and arrows, tomahawks, and many other relics, that he might have them when he reached his happy hunting ground.

A raiding party did not usually carry many rations, and, in case of emergency, a spare horse would be killed and eaten on the spot. The Comanches were not so fond of horsemeat, but when game was not available, it was eaten. There was one taboo: they would never kill their mares. Dogmeat, popular with the Sioux Indians, was taboo among the Comanches. To eat a dog was thought to mean that one would be consumed by his enemy later. Dogs eat human flesh, so they did not relish eating anything that was connected with them. Coyotes were killed for their furs, but they were never eaten or wantonly killed.

There was a superstition about the prairie wolf that made them fear to harm him. Even where wild fowl and fish were plentiful, they were eaten only when food was scarce. Fish was on the taboo list only because of its odor. It was believed that if one ate wild turkey, he would soon become cowardly and run from his enemies, just like the turkey flees from his pursuer. Frogs and swine were also taboo. Frogs were classified with fish, while the swine was associated with mud. The Comanches were smart, for they would eat nothing cooked with hog lard. They were not cannibalistic, though their neighboring Tonkawas practiced this at times. This made them the enemies of the Comanches.

They felt that if one ever tasted human flesh, he would thenceforth develop an insatiable appetite for it. The late winter months of February and March made up the season of scarce food. When food became scarce, the Comanche might be found eating his forbidden food: fish, fowl, terrapins, turtles, snakes, skunks, lizards, and even grasshoppers. There were many lean seasons when roots, hackberries, possum berries, and even barks of trees kept body and soul together.

Their laws were rigid, and they enforced them when violated. They knew no mercy, not even to one of their own band. Their language does not yet suggest anything like gratitude. It is only, "I am glad," not, "I am grateful." The imagination may soar when thinking of how they succumbed to bitter cold, sickness, and calamity. They had their sick and their own ways of doctoring them. Their ministering to the sick was a faith application. When any of the men were sick, the principal chiefs ordered two of the wigwams to be joined together with an opening between. A hole was dug in each of these camps, about two feet deep. In one of them a fire was built, while on the other side of the other tent a lump of mud as large as a man's head, was placed. All around the hole, as well as this lump of mud, the ground is stuck full of willow sprouts. At sunrise, the sick man and musicians enter the camps, and the music is kept up all day. No one must pass close enough to allow his shadow to fall on the camp, or the patient is sure to die, but if everything is done right, he is certain to get well. If he dies, it is attributed to a failure in some of the ceremonies.

In appearance, the Comanches have bright, copper-colored complexions, thin lips, black hair and eyes, but little beard. They have a pronounced aquiline nose. The men are of low or medium stature and well-proportioned. The hard, nomadic life told severely on the women, for they seemed to be ugly and prematurely aged. The men wore moccasins of buckskin and leggings which extended from the upper portion of the thigh to the foot. The garment was close-fitting, for the seam of it ran close in, in order to make the border of the material loose, giving a wide margin of flapping buckskin. A breechcloth or skin was worn and, in cold weather, a buffalo robe or blanket. The dress of the women was a gown or slip that reached from the chin down to the ankles, made usually of elkskins. They tried to ornament them with long fringes of elk's teeth, for these were highly valued among the Indians. Their parade or war regalia had many fantastic designs. Some of the warriors wore a coiffure of buffalo horns, or a hood made of the scalp of the buffalo with the horns attached. Vermilion was much sought after, but colored clay would serve for paint, and each Indian bedaubed himself with his own peculiar design. Bear's claws, horse's hair, mules' tails would be fastened to the hair or the body. Nosepieces of shell, bone, or silver were used, as well as earrings of beads or ornaments. Wristbands of wire were used as ornaments, and served to protect the wrist of the left hand from the slap of the bow string. But on entering battle, these Indians disrobed save for the breechcloth and moccasins. They wanted to be light in their saddles and they never put on anything useless when they mounted their fast horses.

They would make a kind of box out of rawhide, two or three feet long and about twenty inches wide, so it would fit a packsaddle. They cut meat thin, and after hanging it up to dry, they would fold the dry sheets of meat and put it into these rawhide boxes, and place a box on each side of the packsaddle. This was good and palatable, and saved time while traveling. The Indians were fond of tobacco, which they prepared by mixing it with dried sumac leaves and bark. They inhaled the smoke into their lungs and blew it out through their nostrils.

They had very strange charms and were superstitious about many everyday things. The sun played a part in their ritual. The first puff of smoke was offered to the Supreme, the second to the sun, the third to the earth. The first morsel of what they intended to eat was presented to the Great Spirit, and then buried in the ground. Their shields were made in imitation of the sun. They believed that certain birds' skins possessed charms, and the skins of buffalo, bear, and otter were carried into battle. The oil of beaver rubbed on the body was regarded as absolute protection from the rifle ball of the enemy.

The Comanche would not drink from a cup when standing; a mirror was regarded as "bad medicine;" and sticks of wood were never laid across the fire, but instead the end must be inserted and the stick moved up to the fire as the end burned away. They regarded the wolf as a brother who often warned them of impending trouble, and if — when the Indians were on a journey — a wolf jumped up before them, they would change their course and travel no farther in that direction that day. They used steam and vapor baths, and a poultice of prickly pear leaves was applied to check inflammation. If a patient became hopeless, they left him to die, and his death caused an entire village to be moved. They buried their dead in a sitting posture, making a grave or hole just deep enough to hold the corpse, selecting — if possible — a place on a high hill. They had no system of writing, other than drawing crude pictures, and the war and the chase were the themes of the pictures which adorned their shields. Their paints were made from colored chalks or clay, and brushes were tufts of hair from the buffalo. Charcoal served as pencil and barks of trees for canvas.

CHAPTER VII

Preloch

BOUT FOUR YEARS after the capture of Cynthia Ann, or *Preloch,* as she was called by the Comanches, there is some word of her from the white men who saw the girl with the Indians. She was about thirteen years old at this time, for it was in 1840 when Colonel Len. Williams; a Mr. Stoat, a trader; and a Delaware Indian guide named "Jack Harry": found her while exchanging goods with the Indians for their own private gain. They reached the Canadian River and found a group of Comanches whose chief was named *Pa-ha-uka.* Cynthia Ann, or *Preloch,* was with this tribe. Colonel Williams found the Indian family who had adopted her as their daughter and tried to persuade the Indian head of this family to exchange her for the goods which he had. The Indian was very fierce and would accept nothing for the rescue of Preloch, for evidently he valued her too highly. The chief, Pa-ha-uka, urged the Indian to let the white men see her.

Cynthia Ann came and sat down by a tree but would say nothing. She was probably afraid of rough treatment afterward, and had been told to say nothing to the white men. They tried in every way they could to tell Cynthia of her people that had been left behind, and urged her to talk or send some word back to the family. The only response was a quiver of the lips, and these men had to return home without any hope of bringing her back with them to civilization. She probably knew that they would not release her, and there was nothing she could say to the white men to help them understand her position.

As Cynthia Ann grew, she was looked upon as an asset to the Indian who had adopted her. Many braves desired her, and only one who had many horses could obtain her. She was probably large for her age, and her yellow hair, although combed tight and full of grease, was sufficiently different with her white skin to attract the attention of the young men. Her blue eyes set her apart from the other Indian girls, and no doubt she was beautiful, for her mother Lucy had been a lovely woman, and her father Silas came from fine old Virginia stock. So it was that one of the chiefs named Peta Nocona, a Comanche war chief, asked for her. She became the bride of Peta Nocona, and began to take care of the tasks which the offices of his position demanded. It is known that she had three children. The first boy was called Quanah, the second, Pecos, and the third, a little girl, was named Prairie Flower. The tribe of Nocona were called "The Wanderers." They were spoken of as Nocona Indians, for they were a member of the Hasinai Confederacy, and lived southwest of the Neche and Nebedache rivers, until they were forced to the northwest by the settlers from the East.

Almost fifteen years after her capture by the Indians, when Cynthia was about twenty-four years old, some white hunters, and some friends who had known her family, visited the camp of the Comanches in the upper Canadian, and they recognized this girl as Cynthia Ann. Victor M. Ross says:

A party of white hunters, including some friends of her family, visited the Comanche encampment on the upper Canadian and recognizing Cynthia Ann sounded her in a secret manner as to the disagreeableness of this life and urged her to return to the haunts of civilization. She shook her head in a sorrowful negative, and pointed to her little naked barbarians sporting at her feet, and to the great, greasy, lazy buck asleep in the shade near at hand, the locks of scores of scalps dangling at his belt, and whose first utterance upon arousing would be a stern command to his meek, pale-faced wife. Exposure to the sun and air had browned the complexion of Cynthia Ann almost as intensely as the native daughters.

Cynthia Ann retained the smallest remembrance of her people and was now accustomed to the wild life of an Indian. She was married to a young Indian chief, and evidently loved him. There were three children born to this union, and Cynthia Ann felt that they could not be forsaken.

Randolph B. Marcy, in his book *Exploration of the Red River,* in the year of 1852, also spoke of Cynthia Ann. This woman had adopted all the habits and peculiarities of the Comanches. He said they were unable to persuade her to leave the Indians. A dull ear was turned to pleas to go back to the white people. Her life was with the Indians, and she felt it wise to remain. Marcy stated that he had seen and talked with Cynthia Ann's brother, John. He said that John's mother sent him back to seek the release of Cynthia Ann from captivity. This fact is hazy and recorded only by that author.

This span of years had erased from memory many of the facts about her former home, and she now stoically accepted her fate. The Indian chief was followed on his raids, and he would give to Cynthia Ann much of the goods that they captured from the wagon trains. It is possible that the garments she wore were made out of the materials that the Indians took when they raided Linnville. The chief and Cynthia Ann had to flee up the Guadalupe and the Colorado River when the Rangers began to push them back. The white settlers suffered from the attacks of the Comanches, and the Indian women were included in the reprisals of the white man.

Texas was called the country of changing events. During the year of 1836, Cynthia Ann was taken away by her Comanche captors. Ten years after the fall of Fort Parker, where she was captured, the star of Texas was united with the forty-eight of the United States. Texas Rangers and military scouts made many efforts to try to find the whereabouts of the two lost Parker children.

CHAPTER VIII

The Red Plains Riders

PETA NOCONA was a fighting Comanche when Preloch (Cynthia Ann) became his wife. This famous chief was a descendant of an obscure Indian tribe. They were first discovered in the region of Northern Kansas and the central Midwest. The earliest history reveals that these people occupied the section between the upper Platte and the Kansas (Caw) River. These rich hunting grounds are now believed to be occupied by the Kansas Nation. It is thought that this was the early-day residence of the Padoucas, of whom little is known today. These people almost vanished from American history until generations later they sprang up and were called the Red Plains Riders.

These tribes seemed to hold a superiority complex as a race of red men, by the way they designated themselves. Some have believed that the word in the "Caw" language meant "human beings." Evidently, they did not think of other Indian tribes or even the white man as being human. The proud Comanches felt that there was something about their tribe that made them superior, and they called themselves "the people."

Many generations passed before their tribal name was actually known, because the word did not have any root meaning in French, English, or Spanish. It is believed that Mr. Marvin Opler unraveled the mystery with the key that Comanche means "enemy." This was not attained from the white man but from the Ute Indians. The word in Ute had almost the same rendering, "Komantcia." This left a wide field of interpretation, and could be applied to anyone who fought against another. This is evident by the Ute's application of this term to the Cheyennes and the Kiowas, as well as to the Comanches. Some time after 1726, it is believed that the Comanches, endeavoring to push west, were engaged in battles by the Utes. Thus, this roving band of plains riders was given the name "Komantcia" by their enemies.

It is possible that the Spaniards took the word from the Utes and passed it on to the Americans. Some believed that the Spaniards met the Comanches in New Mexico, and that it was here they were given the tribal name "Comanche." The French and Americans did not become acquainted with this famous tribe for several years. A few explorers from both of the nations, who dared to penetrate the great plains, met the Comanches in the eighteenth century. Their original name was not static by this time, for they were called by a Siouan word, "the Padoucas." Such famous explorers as Lewis and Clark, in 1804, heard rumors of them from their Indian scouts.

The historians find that the Comanches began to push south in the middle of the eighteenth cenutry. First the migration was made by a lone tribe, later joined by their famous ally, the Kiowas. Their eating habits and riding skill is good evidence that they were acquainted with the Spanish pony. A keen appetite for buffalo meat, which was their famous food, could be found in large quantities on the high plains area. This is fair proof that they dwelt largely where this game was found. Unlike his redskin brothers, the Comanche was not fond of tall timber nor large bodies of water. It is known that he did eat fish and small game, when he could not obtain the larger animals. His taste was not adapted to the above, because there was not enough blood in the menu. The Comanche adapted himself to the unfriendly nature of the plains and its rigid requirements, in order to live. He learned to face droughts, to withstand severe cold, and to traverse great distances when it was required for his sustenance.

Pushing southward into what is now northern New Mexcio, the Comanches soon annihilated the Pueblos of the Pecos. The Santa Fe territory, by 1838, was almost abandoned by other Indians, because they feared these fierce riders of the plains. The early Spanish frontier settlements of New Mexico soon permitted the red plains riders to pass without molestation. This took the Comanche far into the south on his destructive depredations.

These raids were carried from Durango on the north to Soccoro on the south. The red riders ruled the plains with an unrelenting hand, until they heard of American neighbors who were intruding upon them from the southeast. They became the feared tribe by the Utes, Pawnees, Osages, Tonkawas, Navajos, and even the Apaches. Their horsemanship and brute courage in battle struck terror to the hearts of reds and whites alike. Because of an inbred ingenuity, they soon learned the use of firearms. This gave them an insatiable determination to eradicate other peoples, for they believed that they were the original Americans.

These brutal forays continued until 1795, when there was an unwritten treaty made between the Kiowa and the Comanche. This verbal agreement stood for almost a hundred years. Naked, untrained, armed with the crudest weapons, bloodthirsty with hate, and bold, these Indians fought for their cause — which was the possession of the land where the buffalo roamed. There was only one group of men that put fear into the fighting Comanche, and that was the Texas Rangers.

At the General Council of Texas, when it met at San Felipe de Austin in 1835, these men were selected to fight the Comanche Indians. There were to be three companies. Each group was to be composed of twenty-five men, one to range east of the Trinity, the other between the Trinity and the Brazos, and the last between the Brazos and the Colorado. They were paid a salary of $1.00 per day to move against this common foe. These were the men who would finally push the Comanche out of the plains of Texas. Nocona, the famous plains rider, little knew that the father of Cynthia Ann was a member of the first group of hated Rangers.

These bloody massacres, like the one at Fort Parker, soon called for a dove of peace between the Comanche and the white man. The Indians in their raids had kidnapped many children from the Texans. These were carried back to their villages with the intention of training them in the ways of Indian life. They hoped to induce these children to ride against their own people.

Mirabeau Lamar, the president of the Texas republic, agreed to have a conference with the Comanches. The council was called, and San Antonio de Bexar was the meeting place to discuss these common problems in 1840. At the parley, the war department's representatives made it clear that they would not negotiate a peace treaty until the Comanches were willing to surrender their white captives. The chiefs of the Comanches, one probably being Nocona, were clever and would not agree, but said they would return in two weeks.

General Albert Sidney Johnston, Secretary of War, or-

Cynthia Ann Parker holding her child Prairie Flower, the only picture ever made of her. Her son, Chief Quanah standing by.

The first Baptist Church in Texas built by Daniel Parker.

Interior of this Baptist Church

The blockhouse and gate of Fort Parker, Grosebeck, Texas, originally built
by the Parker clan, now restored.

View of the cabins inside the enclosure of the now restored Fort Parker.

Chief Quanah Parker in his Indian dress.

Quanah Parker and his wife TO-NAR-CY in Indian dress.

Quanah Parker with his three Indian wives.

Children of Quanah Parker, son of Cynthia Ann.

Cynthia Ann Parker's home in Birdville, Texas, after her recapture by Texas Rangers,

Close-up view of Cynthia Ann's home in Birdville. (It was later moved by Amon Carter to Fort Worth as historical monument).

Chief Quanah Parker on his horse at Cache, Oklahoma.

dered Lieutenant Colonel W. S. Fisher of the First Texas Regiment to proceed to San Antonio and take the Indians captive if they failed to bring the prisoners. It was on March 19, 1840, that sixty-five Indians appeared at the council. They had brought only one white girl, whose name was Matilda Lockhart. She told them that there were other captive white children. Colonels Hugh McLeod and W. G. Cooke were sent by President Lamar as commissioners to negotiate with the tribe. Cooke announced that all the Indians would remain in San Antonio as hostages until the white children were returned.

As one of the Indian chiefs arose and went to the door to leave, it was barred by a soldier. The Indian flashed a blade of steel and the soldier fell. Captain Howard tried to grasp the Comanche chief, but he was sorely wounded by the same bloody knife. Just then the bleeding guard fired and the fight began. Knives and muskets wrought a terrible havoc for a few minutes. When the fighting stopped, there were seven white men dead on the floor, with eight others wounded. Thirty-five Indians had met their death.

The peace conference of 1840 ended with the white men holding as prisoners two old Indian men and twenty-seven women and children. The white leaders gave a message to one of the captured squaws, stating that if the Indians would bring all the white captives back, they would make an exchange of prisoners with them. Just one week later, a white flag waved from a nearby hilltop. The Comanches traded twelve white children for twenty-seven of the Indian women and children. But the famous prisoner, Cynthia Ann, was not included in this vital exchange, for she was no longer considered white, but Comanche.

As a result of this trickery, the Comanches again went on the warpath. Without warning, they swept across the Antelope Hills and continued southward as far as Linnville on Matagorda Bay. When the white settlers of Linnville learned through some scouts that the Comanches were headed for their town, they did not stay to fight, but fled by horse and boat across the bay. Nocona and his braves rode up to the town cautiously, the women and children bringing up the rear with their ponies.

The Indians went on a moving spree when they found the whites gone. They loaded the stolen horses with everything from the settlers' homes. Anything shiny and bright attracted their attention, as they collected pots, pans, soap, lard, and utensils. Others were struck by the bright-colored rugs, pillows, and dresses. Everything they did not wish to keep was destroyed amidst a great deal of shouting and screaming. Single file, their horses were led with booty toward their roving camps in the northwest.

The white settlers who had fled called on the Texas Rangers for help. Colonel Burleson and Captain Caldwell organized a group of men and went in search of this moving band. The Indians were not difficult to follow, for along the trail they discarded those things which they considered unimportant. Bolts of cloth, mattresses, pillows, and bedding were strewn over the prairie.

The Indians had several days' start, but the Rangers soon overtook them at Plum Creek. In the distance they could see the Indian camp. The Rangers struck without any warning on August 11, 1840. Nocona and his braves ordered the women and children to move on as fast as their ponies would take them, while the men covered their retreat. Preloch and her two sons mounted their ponies and fled, never thinking that she was, at one time, a hated white. She knew that she must protect her sons, Pecos and Quanah as well as her baby girl, Prairie Flower, from the guns of the white enemy. While the Indians kept the soldiers engaged, she escaped with her ponies that were loaded with the booty from Linnville. The Comanches always scattered for the purpose of confusing the soldiers, and then they regrouped and caught up with the women and children on the trail.

This decisive battle was fought near the present town of Lockhart and ended in defeat for the Comanche. The Comanche continued to roam the plains in small groups, but the trailing white man kept the red plains rider on the move, for fear of sudden attack. The settlers were becoming courageous enough, with the protection of the Rangers, to settle another valley westward. The roving grounds of the red plains riders were being narrowed.

CHAPTER IX

An Engagement at Antelope Hills

THE FIRST MENTION of any record that is found of Nocona is his part in the Indian battle at Antelope Hills. Since Cynthia Ann was his wife, she must have been a witness to this battle, and fled with the Comanches as they took flight toward the Red River country. This was in 1858, when Cynthia Ann was about thirty-two years of age and had lived with the Indians for twenty-three years. The Comanches had their winter resort, which extended south to Pecan Bayou near Brownwood, Texas, to the east along the Brazos near Mineral Wells, and then the open territory west on the clear fork of the Brazos.

This semi-wooded area was full of springs, branches, and creeks, bordered by rivers, and was a virtual winter haunt for game. In severe winters, the buffalo from the plains would migrate into this warm section. It was the deer's natural habitat. It afforded food, water, and protection for the roving Comanches from the severe winter blasts of the high plains. On the west near Albany, Texas, there were low-lying hills covered with wavy grass and scrub mesquites. This was later called the Antelopes' breeding ground. In the north bend of the Clear Fork River, a few miles west of old Fort Griffin, there were some rolling hills that reached 1500 feet, that were later named Antelope Hills. This was a natural run for the roving Comanche, for his blood relished the taste of a good antelope. Many have thought that the mere sport of running them down on horses and sending an arrow through their hearts was one reason that they tasted so delicious. When the Indians made their raids back down to the southeast, they soon learned to resort to the Clear-Fork River country, thence across to the salt fork of the Brazos, up the north Wichita River, and on to the forsaken Pease River.

In 1858, about the first of May, Colonel John S. Ford, or "Old Rip," as he had been nicknamed, commanded a company of about 100 Texas Rangers. Such famous men as Captain S. P. Ross, the father of Gen. L. S. Ross, Bill Tankersley, Bill Pitts, Ed Preston, and a contingent of better than 100 Tonkawa Indians, commanded by their famous chief, "Old Placido," started their march northwestward to take revenge on the cruel Comanche for his reprisal raids. This company of trusted Indians and sturdy whites marched on this campaign against the marauding Comanches, determined to follow them to their lair. It was a stealthy march toward the Canadian River with hopes that, if possible, they might surprise them, and inflict the death blow to their roving, raiding bands. It was a toilsome march of several days over rough terrain when the Tonkawa scouts reported that the Comanche camp was in the immediate vicinity. It was hard to believe, because the Comanches were noted for their sleepless vigilance.

They seemed to be oblivious of any danger, and so the Rangers were unsuspected in their approach. Colonel Ford and Captain Ross took time out to inspect the Indian camps well and to size up their strength. The men stood on a knoll by the old road that runs from Ft. Smith, Arkansas, to Santa Fe, New Mexico, and at this crossroad watched through their field glasses a buffalo slaying by the Comanches in the valley to their north. The Tonkawa scouts went on a hazardous spying expedition that night and completed their dangerous mission without being detected. They marked out every location of the enemy's position. After their return, Colonel Ford mapped out the attack which was to be the next morning, May 12, 1958. The Rangers were to take the left wing, and the reserve, or friendly Indians, were to take the right wing. At the crack of dawn, they planned to make the surprise attack with all military adeptness.

This was possibly one of the most picturesque Indian battles that has ever been fought upon Texas soil. Here were the Comanches on one side and the Tonkawa braves on the other. The surrounding country was a veritable refuge, a nature-made fort for the Comanche Indians. The Comanche Indians had several camps, and the one led by "Old Pohebits Quasho" was the group which the soldiers first attacked. It was not until this skirmish was over that Nocona took over the lead against the white men. Evidently the camp of Peta Nocona and Cynthia Ann was some distance below this first camp where the Rangers had battled at the beginning of the day. "Old Pohebits Quasho" was nicknamed "Iron Jacket," because he was found to be wearing a coat of mail, a curious piece of ancient armor that may have been over 300 years old. It was believed to have been stripped from the body of some unfortunate Spanish knight, perhaps centuries before. It could have been any one of the men of Coronado, De León, or La Salle. But Quasho was now in possession of this coat of mail.

Quasho was a real chief as well as a unique warrior.

He was as ferocious as a leopard, strong as a bear, but as sly as a fox. No Texas Ranger ever questioned his bravery. His own people called him "the big medicine man" or "prophet." He had cast a spell over the superstitious Indians because he had escaped death so many times from rifle fire. His Spanish coat of mail had seemed to make him invulnerable to balls and poisoned arrows aimed at his body. He capitalized on this good luck in the thinking of the braves and became quite a necromancer. He deceived his braves by saying that a puff of his breath would divert the arrow from its course and make it fall harmless at his feet.

Chief Placido of the Tonkawas asked for special privileges for his red warriors, for he wanted to reap vengeance upon their long-time enemies. Colonel Ford granted the chief his request, and the Tonkawas effected a complete surprise attack. The battle was short, sharp, and soon over. Not one Comanche brave of this camp escaped alive, but the women and children were made prisoners. No Comanche brave would surrender, for their savage pride preferred death to the restraints and humiliation of captivity. Not one escaped to bear the sorrowful tidings of this destructive engagement to the rest of their people.

The Rangers came in full view of this hostile camp just after the sun began to shed its rays on the beautiful clay-colored cliffs. They were in a picturesque valley on the opposite side of the river in the immediate vicinity of where the now-famous Antelope Hills are located. The hot blood and the pent-up emotions of the rugged Rangers almost burst into a shout of exultation when this view of battle was presented to their eyes. Colonel Ross speedily suppressed their yells of enthusiasm and warned of impending dangers. Upon investigation they could see a solitary Comanche riding southward. The brave was entirely unaware of any enemy being near at hand. In an instant, they made a dash for him, but he wheeled his pony and fled at full speed back toward the main camp across the river.

The Rangers and the Indian scouts were close on his heels. He dashed across the river, and thus the pursuers found a safe crossing place, for this river was known to be impassable because of the quicksands. He headed his horse into the Comanche village, sounding the cry of warning, and in a moment every Comanche warrior was at his post. They formed a battle line between the women and children and the advancing Rangers. The Rangers halted to take stock of what was before them; then, forming their own lines of battle, they stood in the morning sun, both sides arrayed in full force and facing each other.

Old Placido of the Tonkawas and his braves were placed on the wing and thrown just a little forward. Colonel Ford had hoped to deceive the Comanches as to the character and the number of his attacking force. He had asked both Rangers and Indians to keep their rifles out of sight so that the Comanche would not know the quality of their arms. Chief Pohebits Quasho arrayed himself in full war regalia with his Spanish coat of mail, lance, shield, bow and arrow, and began to yell his commands. His ornate head-dress, decorated with colored feathers with long red flannel streamers, made a ghastly picture when mixed with the ugly war paint that he had smeared on his face. He bravely and gaily dashed up and down between the opposing lines on his beautiful war horse, taunting and challenging his white enemies. As old Quasho rode back and forth, a number of the Rangers tried to shoot at him with their rifles at point-blank range, but without any effect whatsoever. This, of course, stirred the blood of the Comanche warriors, giving them the feeling that their chief was immune to death.

There was even some superstition among the Rangers, who inquired of Captain Ross if he thought it could actually be possible that Old Iron Jacket really possessed a charmed life. Chief Quasho's blood finally reached the boiling point, and, with a few of his braves, he made a daring charge upon the Rangers. He wheeled in his charmed circles, gave a few tiger-like puffs with his breath, and let several arrows fly. Colonel Ford, Captain Ross, and Chief Placido fired back at him, but seemingly without harm. His next "charmed" charge brought him very close to the Tonkawa lines. They had a sturdy Indian called Jim Pockmark, who had a steady nerve and an unerring eye. He raised his rifle, and at the first shot he brought old Pohebits Quasho to the dust. It was a mortal shot from the steady hand of the Tonkawa Indian. The Comanche braves immediately surrounded the form of their fallen chief. It was all in vain, for the spirit of this terror of the Comanches had taken its flight to the happy hunting grounds. Their chief had been mortally wounded.

Time flies fast when incidents like these are happening, so Captain Ross felt that the time had come to charge, and with a deadly phalanx, they made their assault against the Comanche line. The triumphant yell that went up from the Tonkawas, and the enthusiastic shouts and yells of the Rangers, indicated that it was a welcome order. They were ready for battle, and the hour had come. The war whoop of the Comanches rang through those virgin hills, so remote from civilization. It was the battle of the wild — a bloody orgy. The wail of women and the piteous cries of frightened children were heard above the shouts of the enraged combatants. The howling of the frightened dogs, the deadly thud of striking bullets, the sharp reports of rifle and revolver fire, made a discordant symphony that has only been heard in the pits of Hades. It was blended together in an unearthly mass of infernal noise.

The siege was quick and sharp. The fast exchange of

rifle and arrow shots seemed to chill the blood of Rangers and Comanches alike. The heart-rending wail of discomfort from their wives and children threw them off, and they immediately abandoned their lodges and camps to the enemy, and a disorderly retreat ensued. In their retreat they took advantage of every grove of timber, hill, and ravine to make a stand against their hated white killers. This enabled many of their women and children to escape with them. The weird sounds of battle now left the little valley and began to scatter out through the ravines and little creeks. It spread farther and farther, gradually growing fainter and fainter as the pursuit gained distance. It was one o'clock in the afternoon when the force of Rangers and the Tonkawa braves returned from their pursuit of old Quasho's brave marauders. They returned from this siege just in time for a new threatened attack.

The last of the force to return was Captain Ross. He walked up to Colonel Ford and asked him what time of the morning it was. The Colonel told him that it was one o'clock in the afternoon. The danger and the engagement had been so bitter that the flight of time could not be thought about when one was protecting his own life. Captain Ross was surprised to see the Rangers formed again in a line for battle. Colonel Ford just nodded his head and calmly pointed to the hills. Ross turned, and not over a half mile in the distance he saw a force of 500 warriors drawn up in battle array. This force of the Comanches was under the command of Peta Nocona, the young, daring husband of Cynthia Ann Parker. Nocona possibly realized by this time that he was no longer second in command, but the chief of the Indians, since Pohebits Quasho had been slain. A few miles distant with his own braves and women, he had heard the noise of battle, and knowing the rifle fire of the white soldier, he had come to avenge the death of his friend and chief, Pohebits Quasho.

Colonel Ford had successfully routed over 400 Comanches with his company of 225 men. He had done this because he had the feared arms and rifles, while the Indian had only his bow and arrows. But Colonel Ford could not help but think now, as he was confronted by a far stronger force, fresh from their village farther up the Canadian river. He realized that they were crowding the Comanche to the wall, and that now his vehement hate would not stop at anything to drive the paleface back from his Indian campground. There stood Peta Nocona, facing not only the hated white foe, but his ancient Indian enemies, the Tonkawas. They were traitors to the Indian cause and the friends of the white man.

The picture of the captured and destroyed Indian camp before him, with many of its women and children taken prisoners, burned in his heart. He did not feel that he could lose the 400 head of trained horses and the immense quantity of plunder that had been captured and gathered together in their raids. In his anxiety he seemed unconscious of the dangers ahead. Peta Nocona defied the state preparations awaiting him in the valley. He stood serenely waiting for some incautious movement on the part of the Rangers, and then he would avail himself of the opportunity to charge. Peta Nocona had often been called "The Wily Perpetrator" and, like the lynx cat, he was watching for his opportunity when he would spring upon them like a lion from his lair. His plan was to swoop down and annihilate his attackers in one desperate effort. He had forgotten the sagacity of a Texas Ranger, who was only waiting for his charge.

The air was surcharged with an intense feeling; for over an hour each side had been contemplating a charge by the foe. During this time, some of the most majestic operations of Indian fighting ensued between the braves. One side would challenge the combatant to a singlehanded Indian mode of warfare. The Tonkawas took advantage of every tree, ravine, rock, and natural barrior for self-protection. They were carrying six-shooters as well as rifles. Peta Nocona's braves were decked with shields, bow and lance, riding prancing steeds like the medieval knights of old. He displayed every gorgeous colored finery and pomp that could be found on a savage. These Comanche warriors would gallop to a halfway point between the lines, give a defiant war whoop, shake their shields, and challenge the enemy to a single combat. This was more than the Tonkawa brave could endure. They were compelled to accept such challenges by their more expert adversaries. The consequences were fatal to them, and Colonel Ford ordered the Tonkawas to stop answering these savage challenges.

Old Chief Placido did not like this order at all but, like the good Indian that he was, he conducted himself throughout the engagement with the bearing of a good soldier. Colonel Ford, in describing this foray, said these combats took him back to his studies in college in the history of the combats in the days of chivalry, when the knights engaged in jousts and tournaments. This is possibly the last exhibition of such scenic gallantry among the red man. The Comanches' feats of horsemanship were something to marvel at, and they used their shields and lances with great and incredible dexterity.

This type of display could not last forever, for both sides were bloodthirsty and anxious to get the battle over. Chief Placido and his warriors were ordered by Colonel Ford to advance upon the enemy. He thought if possible he would draw them from their stronghold into the valley. This would give the Rangers an opportunity to charge. It worked out just as he had desired. The Tonkawas advanced; the Comanches could no longer stand still. They came in the right direction, and the Rangers were ready to deliver their charge. Before going into this battle, the friendly Tonkawas had been asked by the Colonel to remove the white badges from their heads. These badges had been used to identify the Tonkawas from the other Indians, so that the enraged white man would not make a mistake. The Comanches had a veritable hatred for the Tonkawas, and these white badges served as targets.

By this time, the Rangers were able to identify their friendly allies from their foes. When the Comanches discovered this, they seemed perplexed and began immediately to recoil. At the very intimation of the retreat, the Rangers advanced first in a trot, next a gallop, and then a headlong charge with pistols blazing. Lieutenant Nelson followed in rapid succession and made a skillful charge, cutting off the enemy's left flank. This broke the Comanche line, which always seemed to throw him into a rout — man after man, horse after horse, each depending upon his ability and skill to outrun or to overtake the enemy. Peta Nocona made a few stands, but he was driven back wherever he tried it. He finally found a timbered ravine, where he put up his most determined resistance. Chief Placido lost one of his gallant warriors in this ravine, and young George Pascal was wounded. Many of the Comanches were left dead in the ravine, and several of the wounded kept pushing on. The Rangers really routed them at this point, but they continued the pursuit with the intent of taking the women and children prisoners.

Peta Nocona was a military genius among the Indians. His commanding qualities often revealed his military strategy on the field. Peta Nocona successfully covered his retreat and allowed the women and children to make their escape. By four in the afternoon, both cmen and horses were exhausted, the Colonel ordered a halt, and they started back toward the first Indian village. It had been an eventful day for both warriors and Rangers. Old Chief Placido and his Indians had fought like demons. They were hard to restrain, because they wanted to reap their vengeance on the hated Comanches.

It was estimated that seventy-five Comanches lost their lives in this bitter engagement. Among the Rangers, two had been killed and six wounded. Old Pohebits Quasho's trophies, his coat of mail, headdress, bow, lance, and shield were taken by Colonel Ford and deposited in the Indian Archives at Austin, Texas. Ross said that Chief Placido of the Tonkawas was placed that day among the heroes of Texas by his gallant fighting. He later fell a victim to the revengeful Comanches, who never forgot the part he played in their defeat. He was assassinated by his enemies on the reservation near Fort Sill, Oklahoma.

Cynthia Ann Parker rode from this bloody battle with her infant daughter, Prairie Flower, pressed to her bosom. Her two sons, now about the ages of ten and twelve, were riding ponies by her side in the escape from the hated white man. Although nothing but white blood flowed in her veins, she was as fearful of capture at the hand of the hated white man as any Comanche who rode with that band of Indians. This was far different from the day of the massacre of old Fort Parker, when she was hoisted away from her much-loved home by a Comanche brave, to face the dangers and hardships of the Indian way of life. Twenty-three years with the Indians had erased from her mind the love of the white people and the former fear of the Indians.

CHAPTER X

Cynthia Ann Captured at Pease River

THE VICTORY at Wichita Mountains by Captain Ross cooled the Comanches down considerably. They were less hostile for some time and feared to penetrate very deep into the nearby communities. In the late 1859's, the frontier became disturbed again. The plainsmen were obliged to stand daily in defense of their common foe, the roving Comanche. The savages did not pillage in large bands; but in small bodies continually attacked the unarmed and unprotected.

The cowboy on the trail never knew at what moment the Comanches would spring from behind a bush or a rock and strike the fatal blow. They hit fast and ran faster, until they arrived back into their safe retreat. Nocona, in the early fall of 1860, began to stir the leaves and move southward. With his pack train of horses and mules, with rude baskets fastened on two poles and tied to the saddle, they started south with the wild geese. These crude carts were made of two poles tied on each side of the saddle; the ends dragging the earth were the chariots for the little ones to ride in. Tepees and bundles of robes were transported in the same manner: by dragging the two poles tied to the pack mules. On these survey invasions, a group of warriors, ready for action, always rode in advance; others scattered out ahead to kill game for the sustenance of the band. These forward scouts were rather cunning, for they had the eye of an eagle to catch every movement of danger. It made a formidable pack train that was strung out for miles, for even the children had their own ponies, and were taught to ride at an early age. They established their camp near the sun-painted red cliffs of the Pease River. The Indians named it "Prairie Dog Town River." The Pease River valley with its cliffs afforded much protection from the blue northers for the comfort of the people as well as of their stock. There was water, dry grass, and plenty of mesquite wood for fire. This also put them in striking distance of the white settlements and provided them with ample opportunity for horse stealing in the country to the south. The Noconas were known as *Det-sanu-kas* or "bad campers" because they were always on the move and never had time to make good camps or to improve their equipment.

The coming of the autumn frost always stirred the blood of a Comanche brave, making him eager to be on the march. Peta Nocona, in 1860, headed his raiding party through Parker County. This county had been named in honor of his wife's own uncle, Issac Parker. It might have given Peta more respect for the citizens, or he may have reasoned that, on her account, he had some inherited rights. When the moonlight nights came, and he drew a diagram of his next itinerary, it always included Parker County. From Parker County he went on toward the flourishing communities toward the southwest border of the Texas wilds. He was indomitable and fearless, and left his trail of depredations wherever he went. These thieving expeditions, with their marauding and destruction, were carried to the West as far as Weatherford, Texas. The much-loved uncle of Cynthia Ann was a resident of the little town at this time. He never dreamed that the chief of these ruthless savages who were bringing terror and death to the settlers could be the husband of his long-lost niece, Cynthia Ann Parker.

Strange, indeed, to think that the blood of the murdered Parkers and that of this wild Peta Nocona would one day merge in a chief of the proud Comanches. The Comanches boasted of their superiority in strength and intellect, and their claim of superiority over other Texas tribes would not be questioned in the realm of courage. Nocona became so notorious that the settlers began to demand protection and help. These atrocities and depredations demanded that the government set out an expedition for the protection of the settlers and the emigrants. A regiment was organized and sent out under Colonel M. D. Johnson, but it proved of little benefit to the state. It cost the government a nominal sum, but they failed to find one Comanche, and so they returned.

Strangely enough, the command itself was followed by the wily Comanches who would stampede their horses at night. Many of the soldiers therefore reached the settlement on foot, suffering from cold and exposure. The next attempt was made when Governor Sam Houston appointed Captain Sul Ross, a young graduate who had just returned to Texas. He organized a company of sixty men, with forty Rangers and twenty soldiers, to hunt down and destroy the band of Comanches. Captain Ross was in command with a little Irishman by the name of Tom Killiheir as first lieutenant. The late F. M. Peveler of Weatherford was eighteen years old at this time, and was also a member of the party.

They left Camp Cooper, which was forty miles west of

Fort Belknap, and received from Colonel Johnson all the government property that his regiment had failed to use. This was a small force to afford frontier protection against such an uncanny foe as Peta Nocona. Captain Ross soon became tired of the hit-and-run tactics of the Comanches, as they left their destruction behind without an opportunity to catch the destroyer. He determined to follow the Indians into their fastnesses and carry the war to their own hunting grounds.

Borrowing a detachment from the Second Cavalry under Captain N. G. Evans, he took them with his own men and organized a posse to trail them to their lair. This small force was augmented by seventy volunteer cowboys under the command of the brave old frontiersman Jack Cureton, of Bosque County. These patriots of the brush country were tough and alert. They had no hope of pay or reward, but left their homes defenseless and their families to face hardships, in order to avenge the sufferings of their neighbors. They loaded their pack mules down with needed supplies and started on the march toward the Indian country.

They rode hard for several days and part of the nights, marching and following the trail up the Pease River. Here they found fresh signs where women and children had gathered hackberries and skinned a polecat. Just over the ridge in the valley of a small creek, numerous ravens were making a great noise. The raven is allied to the crow family, and somewhat more boisterous. Frontiersmen know that at the smell of blood or sight of raw meat the ravens congregate in great numbers with much squawking. The soldiers knew by this that the Indian buffalo hunters were nearby. This was on the 18th of December, 1860, and they were suspicious that Indians were in the vicinity. Several buffalo herds had come running by them from the north, a sign that a hunt was in progress in that direction.

Ross halted the command, moved stealthily through the arroyos to some high points, so he might take in the country below. Hitting one of the tops of these sandhills, the captain found fresh pony tracks to indicate that the Indian scout had just left. Ross galloped forward a mile to a higher point, and when he reached the top of the sand knoll, found to his surprise, that the Comanches were not over 200 yards away, spread out in the valley. A small, clear stream was winding through their camp. It looked like a happy situation, being protected from the north wind that was blowing by the clay-colored cliffs; for a blue norther was whipping up a little sandstorm that cut him off from their sight.

The captain stood there unobserved, planning in his own mind his next move. Standing concealed, he signaled to his men to approach quietly on their horses, so they would not be detected by the Indians. When he turned again, he was surprised to find that they were busy packing up their mules in preparation to leave. Immediately some of the Indians mounted and began to move off northward to the plains. The detachment of Second Cavalry had outmarched the citizen command of the army and left Ross with about sixty men. In making preparation for the attack, one sergeant and twenty men were sent at a gallop behind a chain of sandhills to cut off their retreat to the northwest, while — with forty men — Ross was to make the charge. The Indians did not suspect that the white men were so near the camp.

The attack was so sudden that a great number of Indians were killed before they could prepare for defense. The others fled right into the arms of the sergeant and his men. The Comanches, finding themselves completely surrounded, began to flee, every man to his own way, but were hotly pursued by the Rangers and the tough cowboys. Peta Nocona was the chief of the band and a warrior of great repute. He tried to make a sly getaway. Completely forgetting

the others, he mounted a fleet steed, with a fifteen-year-old
girl behind him, and fled. Behind was Cynthia Ann Parker,
with her two-year-old baby girl mounted on another slender
pony, as she followed up a shallow creek.

Captain Ross and Tom Killiheir pursued these fleeing
fugitives. Killiheir, after about a mile of chase, ran up by
the side of Cynthia Ann's horse and was in the act of
shooting her when she held up her baby girl and stopped
her horse. Captain Ross kept right on after the chief, and
about half a mile on, he came within twenty yards of him.
He fired his pistol point-blank, striking the girl near the
heart and killing her instantly. He had supposed that it was
a man, for she rode like a brave, and only her head was
visible above the buffalo robe. The same shot would have
killed the chief, but for the shield that he was wearing,
which covered his back. The girl, in falling from the horse,
pulled the chief off with her, but like a lynx cat he landed
on his feet and immediately steadied himself. The captain's
horse, running at full speed, almost ran over him, when the
horse was caught with an arrow which caused him to start
bucking. Ross had great difficulty in remaining in the saddle,
and he narrowly escaped several poisoned arrows that came
in quick succession from Nocona's bow. Providence alone
could have saved Captain Ross from his fate, but like a
desperate man he fired wild-eyed with his pistol in his left
hand, holding to the pommel of the saddle, and by shooting
carefully he broke Nocona's right arm at the elbow.

This left the chief helpless and merciless in the face of
a hardy Texas Ranger. When his horse quieted down, the
Ranger, still fearing Peta Nocona, fired two shots through
the body of the chief. The renowned warrior deliberately
stalked over to a small tree; leaning his body up against it,
he began to sing the death song of the Indian. Ross' Mexican servant and cook, named Antonio Martinez, soon caught

up with his captain, and having been a captive of the Comanches, he spoke their language fluently. Through him, Ross summoned Chief Nocona to surrender. The Indian treated such commands with contempt and showed it by trying to thrust Ross through with a lance in his left hand. Ross looked upon him with pity and had to admire the daring courage of old Comanche Peta Nocona.

He did not have a chance to escape. His Indian band was scattered like antelope, his wife and baby stood as captives in his sight, but he was undaunted by his fate, preferring death to slavery. Ross commanded the Mexican to end his misery by a charge of buckshot from the gun he carried. The captain took all the belongings of the chief, and such evidence as he could acquire, and sent them to Governor Houston to be deposited in the archives of the state in Austin.

When he turned back to Cynthia Ann, he found Killiheir cursing bitterly because he had run his pet horse so hard and captured nothing but an old squaw. The squaw was very dirty and unkempt, and her person was clothed with scanty garments. But when the captain looked into her face, he was astonished, and said to Killiheir, "This is a white woman." — for Indians do not have blue eyes. They took the squaw and went back to the Indian village where the men were assembling the spoils and where they had corralled a large number of Indian ponies. On their way Ross discovered a nine-year old Indian boy hiding in the grass like a coyote. He began crying, expecting to be killed, but Ross put him behind him on his horse and took him back to McLennan County, where he lived and grew into manhood, never returning to his people.

Starting Cynthia Ann on her journey back to the white settlements, it was noted that she cried continually. They tried to solace her through the Mexican interpreter who told her that they realized that she was one of their own people and that they did not intend to harm her. She finally revealed her sorrow by saying that two of her boys were with her when the fight began, and she was distressed because she feared they both had been killed by the white men. The men told her they had killed no Indian children, and it is known that both of them escaped. The one was named Pecos and nicknamed Peanut, and the other one became the famous Indian chief, Quanah. It is not known exactly how long the boys wandered on the plains, but it is known that Pecos died a number of years later, while Quanah grew up in an adopted tribe of the Comanches.

Captain Ross, day by day, quizzed Cynthia Ann about the circumstances of her capture by the Indians and the history of her life with the Comanches. She answered in a fairly sensible manner. Ross could not help but believe that her story and the detailed facts corresponded with the events he had heard of the massacre at Parker's Fort. Belief rose in his heart that this might be the long-missing Cynthia Ann Parker. When he returned to Fort Cooper, he sent Cynthia Ann and her child, Prairie Flower, to the ladies, where she could receive help and attention, so desperately needed at this time. They bathed her and gave Cynthia Ann and her child suitable clothes, for all she had were rags and a buffalo robe to wrap around her. They washed her hair and tried to comfort her as best they knew how. Ross immediately sent word to Colonel Isaac Parker, who lived near the town of Weatherford, to come to Fort Cooper and see if this woman was his long-lost niece. When Isaac Parker arrived, the Mexican interpreter was sent with Colonel Parker and together they went to the home of Captain N. G. Evans, the commandant at Fort Cooper and husband of Mrs. Evans, who had been taking care of Cynthia Ann.

This sun-tanned, blue-eyed woman, with hard, coarse,

lines of care in her face, had no resemblance to the nine-year-old Cynthia Ann who was hoisted away from Parker's Fort twenty-five years before. The questioning started by her father's own brother, in hopes of electrifying her memory and thus gaining some evidence of her identity. They talked to her of the childhood scenery around Parker's Fort, the spring, the grapevines, the trails to her home, but they seemed to find no response. They talked of the terrible massacre of old Fort Parker and the atrocities committed by the Comanches. They called the names of her father and mother, and her brothers and sister and other relatives, in hopes that they might catch a gleam of recognition in her blue eyes. Those eyes seemed to be gazing into blank space and traveling afar where she had roamed with a Comanche Indian band. A slain Comanche chief and two missing boys seemed to occupy the thinking of her mind and the devotion of her heart. She was an Indian, stolid, serene, and complacent in her regard to pleasing other people. Her uncle Isaac at last arose almost in despair. Her answers were too vague, and he could not be certain. Doubt filled his mind and he kept saying, "It might be Cynthia Ann. It pieces together . . . " — but then, in a low voice, he was heard to say, "Maybe we are wrong — poor Cynthia Ann." Then, out of the dark past, like a looming arrow, something pierced the stolid heart of this Comanche princess. Her bewildered mind awoke and she heard the faint echo of a mother's voice crying, "Cynthia Ann — Cynthia Ann." The scowl on her face turned to a faint light and could almost be called a smile. Falteringly and brokenly, she framed the forgotten words, "Cynthia — me Cynthia," and pressed her hand over her heart.

CHAPTER XI

Cynthia Ann Returns

LEAVING HER REAL HOME as a bonny blue-eyed lassie, nine years of age, and then returning as a dark, savage-like woman of thirty-four years, is a paradox indeed. The innocent little girl had lived a hundred lives in a period of twenty-four years with the Indians. Only the inscrutable mind of God will ever know the varied, savage, and horrible experiences she had with these roving Comanches. The providence of God protected her, but the experiences of the dusty trail molded her personality. Her emotions were put into a Comanche mold, her mind was made keen by the Comanche ingenuity, and her future detemined by her love for the Indian way of life.

The wagon journey home from Fort Cooper was not as long as the journey of an awakening mind that had been dulled by excruciating experiences. It was like a mind that had been drugged by an anesthetic, which awakens slowly as the toxin is removed and fresh life injected. The brain had become numbed with horrors, the heart had become hard through suffering, the will almost impenetrable by cruel resistance. Her distorted personality did not chill the love of an overjoyed uncle, who came to Fort Cooper to discover her.

Pioneer love for a kinsman was not easily broken, and would go its full lengths in endeavoring to help this poor woman. She and her baby, Prairie Flower, who was about two years old at this time, went with Mr. Isaac Parker to his home in Birdville. This home was about seventy-five years old at this time. It was a double log cabin with an opening in the center. There was a large wide porch, and a fireplace inside. It was here that Cynthia Ann was brought. This cabin is still in existence today, and may be seen just as it stood in 1860, when it became the home of Cynthia Ann.

Amon G. Carter of Fort Worth had it carefully removed to his country estate, "Shady Oaks," on Lake Worth, and it was rebuilt, log for log, just as it stood in Birdville. The old bedsteads, marble-covered dressers, pictures, and furnishings are just as they were when they were used by the Parker family. This was strange to Cynthia Ann, and the surroundings were different from the wild Indian life that she had lived. It has been said that more than once she mounted a horse and tried to escape, but all was in vain, as she was brought back.

The Parkers took her on a trip to Austin when the Texas convention was in session. She was received well in Austin, and several of the Texas ladies accepted her very graciously. They dressed her neatly and took her into the convention hall. It was learned later that she was greatly alarmed when she entered this meeting place, for Cynthia Ann believed it was a council of chiefs who were passing judgment on her life. The ladies and their husbands reassured her that she was among Texas friends. It was no easy task to take this wild captive of the Comanches and train her to the customs of civilization. She was very morose at times, and although she had her baby girl, she grieved for her two boys. Prairie Flower was given the name "Tecks Ann," although her Indian name was *Topasannah*.

Gradually the English language came back to her mind, bringing back the incidents of her childhood. It had been promised that, if she would learn the Engish language and adapt herself to her new home, she would be permitted to visit the Indian people again. She was granted $100 a year for five years, beginning in January of 1861. Since she was living with Isaac Duke Parker, he was appointed as her guardian. Cynthia Ann was granted one league of land to be located anywhere she might choose. This act, granting her a pension and the land, was passed by the Texas Legislature in April 8, 1861. It was for the support of Cynthia Ann, and also for aid in the education of her child. The following is a copy of the act by which she received this help:

An Act Granting a Pension to Cynthia Ann Parker

Section 1.   Be it enacted by the legislature of the State of Texas that Cynthia Ann Parker, of Tarrant County, Texas, be, and she is hereby entitled to receive from the State of Texas, a pension of one hundred dollars per annum for five years, commencing the 1st day of January, 1861, to be paid quarterly, as herein after specified, and the sum of one hundred dollars is hereby appropriated out of any money in the treasury not otherwise propriated to pay said pension the first year, ending the 1st day of January, 1862.

Section 2.   That the County Court of Tarrant County, shall on application, appoint a guardian for said Cynthia Ann Parker, who shall give a bond to the Chief Justice of Tarrant County, in the sum of five hundred dollars, conditioned for the faithful application of said pension to the support of said Cynthia Ann Parker, and for the support and education of her child, and upon the production of the certificate of the State, certifying that said guardian has qualified and his

bond approved, the Treasurer shall pay the said pension to
the said guardian of his order.

Section 3.   That this act take effect from its passage. Approved April 8, 1861.

An Act Donating Land to Cynthia Ann Parker

Section 1.   Be it enacted by the legislature of the State of
Texas that the Commissioner of the General Land Office be,
and he is hereby authorized and required to issue to Cynthia
Ann Parker, a certificate for one league of land, to be located, surveyed and patented as other land certificates, upon any of the vacant and unappropriated public land of
the State of Texas.

Section 2.   That the title to the land granted by the first
section of this act shall vest in Isaac Duke Parker and Benjamin Parker in trust for the said Cynthia Ann, and in the
execution of said trust, they shall be governed by the laws
now in force, or which may hereafter be enacted, in relation
to guardian of property and persons of minors; provided
that said title shall not vest in said trustees or said Cynthia
Ann, until trustees give bond and security as required by
said law in relation to guardians of the property and persons
of minors.

Section 3.   That this act take effect and be in force from
and after its passage. Approved April 8, 1861.

Since Cynthia Ann seemed to be so unhappy at Birdville,
and since her own brother Silas Junior was willing to take
her into his care in the year of 1862, she moved from the
home of this uncle to the home of her brother in Van Zandt
County in eastern Texas. Silas M. Parker was one of the
two children who escaped the massacre on May 19, 1836.
Cynthia Ann was thirty-four at this time, and thus her
younger brother would be about twenty-eight. Her mother

had evidently died, for there has been no mention of her. If she had been living, Lucy Duty Parker would have been the first one to attempt to see her daughter. Silas Jr. had secured land to the north of Fort Parker and had lived there with his family. Thus, there is an amendatory act on the books of the Texas legislature in the change of guardianship for Cynthia Ann:

An Act Amendatory of an Act Supplementary to the Second Section of an Act Granting a Pension to Cynthia Ann Parker, Approved April 8, 1861.

Section 1.   Be it enacted by the legislature of the State of Texas that the second section of the above recited act shall hereafter read as follows:

Section 2.   That Silas M. Parker of Van Zandt County is hereby constituted as agent for Cynthia Ann Parker, formerly of Tarrant and now of Van Zandt County, and on giving bond in the sum of four hundred dollars to the Chief Justice of Van Zandt County, conditioned for the faithful application of said pension to the support of said Cynthia Ann Parker, and for the support and education of her child Topasannah, and upon the production of the certificate of the clerk of the County Court of Van Zandt County, to the Treasurer of the State of Texas, certifying that said agent has given bond as required by this act the said treasurer shall pay the said pension to the said agent or his order.

Section 3.   That this act take effect and be in force from and after its passage. Approved January 8th, 1862.

It was about the time when they promised Cynthia Ann that they would take her back to find her two lost Indian children that the Civil War broke out in the North and South. This occupied the mind and strength of Texas for four long years. Texas was not in the midst of the fighting, and there was not much bloodshed on the soil of Texas, but the blockade cut off the supplies and many of the men left to fight for the South. This required the women to turn again to the spinning wheels and the looms to make their cloth. They were amazed at the skill that Cynthia Ann revealed in this work, and she soon proved to be worth her keep in the spinning of cloth and the platting of rugs. She was taught to use the old churn and to cook like other white woman.

Before they brought Cynthia Ann to east Texas, she visited Fort Worth, and it was at that time that a photographer persuaded her to go with him and have a picture taken. This picture was taken with her baby daughter, Prairie Flower. The original is today in the collection of Texas history at the Baylor Library in Waco, Texas. In later years, Quanah advertised in the Fort Worth *Gazette* for a picture of his mother, and in answer to his request, Colonel Ross sent a copy of this picture to him. Quanah's friend Burnett had a painting made from the small photograph, and Quanah hung it on the walls of his home in Cache, Oklahoma.

The latter part of Cynthia Ann's life, after she was captured, was sad and lonely. As far as Cynthia Ann was concerned, she had altogether lost her identity, for in her own mind she was a full-blooded Indian. She had assumed their habits, ways and customs, married Peta Nocona, borne his children, and become a slave and burden-bearer for him, as was the custom of all Indian wives. But after the death of her Indian brave and her separation from her two Indian boys, she refused to be comforted. She had lost her husband, and was left alone with her little girl, prisoners of her deadly enemies. It is said by those who were with her in these days that she never smiled again.

She possessed the maternal love that is always found in the Indian mother. Day by day she cherished the hope of reclaiming her two boys, who still lived with the Comanches. Providence was not so kind, for while the Civil War was still being fought, the little brown runabout girl who chattered more English than Comanche, was taken out of her arms by a fever. Her Indian name was Topasannah, but she was called "Little Prairie Flower" and "Tecks Ann." Now more than ever she seemed to have one desire, and that was to go back, hunt and find her two boys. They buried the little girl in the old Asbury graveyard, which is about eight miles from the present town of Ben Wheeler. Poor Cynthia Ann grieved over the loss of the child, and so moved to Anderson County to be with her sister and brother-in-law, whose name was Ruff O'Quinn.

The last days of her life were spent in Henderson and Anderson counties. The O'Quinns, McSpaddens, Palmers, Anglins, Duty,s, Starrs, and Allisons were all related to her by blood. They lived in the northeastern part of this county, and later some of them lived in the southeastern part. She died of a broken heart on Caddo Creek at the sawmill owned by her relative O'Quinn, near the line of Henderson and Anderson counties. The acts of kindness given her by the white man were the greatest punishment that could have been inflicted upon her. She had only one hope and longing in her heart, and it seemed to be the only one to give her solace; for she was told that after the Civil War she could go back home to the Indian tribe and her two little boys and live with them. But she died before the war ended in the year of 1864, when only thirty-four years old.

Cynthia Ann, the Comanche princess, never had the privilege of rejoining her beloved people. It was a sad ending of an eventful life. No one has ever been conscious of the part this girl played as a mediator between the sturdy pioneer and the enraged Comanche in the life of her son

Quanah. T. J. Cates of Ben Wheeler has this to say concerning Cynthia Ann:

"I well remember Cynthia Ann Parker and her little girl, Tecks Ann; she lived at the time about six miles south of Ben Wheeler, with her brother-in-law, Ruff O'Quinn, near Slater's Creek. She looked to be stout and weighed about 140 pounds, well-made, and liked to work. She had a wild expression and would look down when people looked at her. She could use an ax equal to a man and she liked to work, and disliked a lazy person. She was an expert in tanning hides with the hair on them, or plaiting or knitting either ropes or whips. She thought her two boys were lost on the prairie after she was captured and would starve to death. This dissatisfied her very much, and she wanted to go back to the Indians. She would take a knife and hack her breast until it would bleed, then put the blood on some tobacco and burn it, and cry for her lost boys. Almost every Sunday my wife would carry the little Indian girl, Tecks Ann, visiting. She was pretty and smart, and was about three years of age the last time we saw her. She died and was buried in old Asbury graveyard about eight miles south of Ben Wheeler. Poor Cynthia Ann was grieved over the loss of her child and she then moved to Anderson County, where she soon died of la grippe. She was an open-hearted, good woman, and always ready to help somebody."[1]

Cynthia Ann was buried in old Fosterville Cemetery in Henderson County, Texas. The Fosterville Cemetery is four or five miles south of the city of Poynor. To reach it, one turns south at Poynor for one and a half miles, and then left on a woodland road. But the story does not end with this forgotten grave, for Cynthia Ann never forgot her Indian sons, and they in turn did not forget their white

---

1 Cates, T. J., *Cynthia Ann Parker*, Edgewood Journal; June, 1918.

mother. Forty-six years later, in the year 1910, her son came after her body and took it back to be with the Indian people. But the story must go backward and the threads picked up to see how the lives of the Indian boys that were left on the plains in 1860 were woven into the future of the Comanche history. They had a great heritage, for they had an Indian chief for their father and a white woman for their mother, and through the blood of Peta Nocona and that of Cynthia Ann Parker, they became a force in the fate of the Comanche Indian and the relationship of peace that was needed to bind these two races together. Quanah was that mediator, and he was the boy that Cynthia Ann longed for as she died in a lonely cabin in the woods of east Texas.

CHAPTER XII

Quanah Parker

HE TWO CHILDREN of Peta Nocona and Cynthia Ann Parker, who were left without mother or father on the banks of the Pease River, were Quanah and Pecos. It is well known that she had two sons who escaped her fate of being captured by the white soldiers. This was in the cold month of December, 1860, and knowing that they would probably never see their mother again, they were discouraged. They talked around the campfire as to how they might rescue her from the hated white people. Quanah, at this time, was about fourteen, for it is believed that he was born about 1854. The other brother, Pecos, died and did not live to mature manhood. Cynthia Ann had named him Pecos, but sometimes he was called by his nickname, "Peanut." He died on the plains before his mother.

Quanah was a Nocona Indian, which means wanderer, but after his father, Peta Nocona, was killed, he was adopted and cared for by the Cohoites. He was made a sub-chief because of his bravery. From the year 1860 until 1874, a period of fourteen years, he was with this tribe, wandering over the plains of Texas. He went on his first raid on the Santa

Fe trail. They were after horses and mules, which they found in Texas, but they were not able to find much of the goods which they needed.

It was in 1867 that the president sent word that there would be a council for the Indians, and that problems would be discussed and presents presented. This message came from Kansas, but the Comanche tribes received the word and met with the other tribes northward on the Nescatunga River. It was near this river that they camped. It was a great sight to see the Indian camps pitched as far up and down as the eye could see. There were Kiowas and the Plains Indians, the Arapahoes, as well as various bands of Comanches. Here were all the tribes with more than 700 lodges. General Harney and General Augus were the leaders for the white government, with the help of Vananiel G. Taylor. The white men camped on the hilltop, and wagons were brought from the East laden with gifts which the Indians would enjoy. They had brown sugar, tobacco, boxes of crackers, tin cups, pans, coffee, bright blankets, suits, clothes, beads, chains, bracelets, mirrors, ribbon, paints, saddles, and bridles. It was here that Quanah learned the story of his mother's return to her white people and the sad news of her death.

It was agreed by the Indian chiefs that all the land south of the Arkansas belonged to the Kiowas and Comanches. The peace was made, and the Cheyennes and Arapahoes were to have the lands south from the North Canadian to the Washita, and the Kiowas and Comanches from the Washita to the Red River. The Chichasaw lands were to be on the east, with the North Fork as their western limit. Quanah was at this time with the Quahadis group of the Comanches. The Comanches were divided into several bands, each band giving loyalty to their own tribal group. There were the Costcheteghtkas, or buffalo-eaters; the Peneteghtkas, or honey-eaters; the Nokonees, or wanderers; the Yampericos, or root-diggers;

and the Quahadas of the staked plains, the antelope-users.

The Quahada band had for many years been isolated from the tribe, for they refused to enter into the Medicine Lodge Treaty of 1867, by which the Comanches, Kiowas, Apaches, Cheyennes, and Arapahoes were assigned to reservations. They roamed outside of any reservation. All the cities of Texas were open to their bloody and frequent raids. This was the wildest and most hostile band of Comanches of the Texas borderland. They made their headquarters in Blanco Canyon, which was about the headwaters of the Pease River.

In 1867 to 1871, the band was out under Quanah, moving about from place to place, but always returning to the headwaters of the Pease River. They raided in the plains, striking far into the Texas frontier past the forts of Richardson, Belknap, Bliss, and Stockton. They rode across the Pease River and on to Gainesville. Here they raided for the horses and mules, and then quickly set out for their distant homes. Word was taken to Fort Richardson, and a company of soldiers quickly organized; fast travel found them soon on the Red River. The white men did not follow across the river, but there was a battle and one of the Indian chiefs was killed.

On one raid made on April 24, 1869, the Indians stole a number of horses from the settlers on Sanchez Creek. There were sixteen Indians in the band under Quanah. This was in Parker County, over some of the trails made by his father ten years before. Quanah wore a blue Yankee coat with brass buttons, which he was supposed to have secured from some soldiers at the agency at Fort Sill. Seven active young men, Sam Newberry, Tom Cox, Milt Ikard, Will Gray, Elbert Doss, John Doss, and Bose Ikard gave chase. Well mounted, but armed only with six-shooters, they overtook the Indians in a running fight near Mineral Wells. The redskins abandoned their horses, and, with guns, fought behind the rocks. They killed Elbert Doss, and forced the boys to retreat. It is to Sam Newberry and Milt Ikard that the information of this story comes. They knew they had shot several Indians. In the running fight, the boys with the six-shooters had the advantage, but when the Indians left their horses and took shelter behind rocks, it was too dangerous to follow them. Sam Newberry knew he shot one Indian off his horse, and he saw him crawl behind a rock. He also got one shot at Quanah. Milt Ikard knew Quanah later in Oklahoma, and they discussed this fight. Quanah admitted that they had nine men out of sixteen either killed or wounded, and that the Indians lost twelve horses. The body of Elbert Doss was carried back on Newberry's horse to his family.

In August, 1871, General R. S. Mackenzie was determined to pay his attention now to the Indians of the Texas Panhandle. The Indians would hide in the fastnesses, the breaks, and small canyons of the "Staked Plains." It was in September that they left Fort Richardson to punish the Quahadas. They reorganized at Camp Cooper on the Ketumseh's Creek, a tributary of the Clear Fork of the Brazos, about five miles from Fort Griffin. Robert E. Lee built this post some years before the Civil War. On September 25, some eight companies of the Fourth Cavalry and two companies of the Eleventh Infantry, with about twenty Tonkaway scouts, were in camp near Fort Griffin. On that night, a band of Indians under Quanah came into Murphy's ranch, about twenty miles from the post, and ran off a herd of 120 cattle and thirteen horses.

The white men left their bivouac and started, with about 600 men and 100 pack horses, to hunt for Quanah. The Indian scouts who were called "Tonks" were far in advance, looking for trails. The soldiers sang and the words rang out, "Come home, John, don't stay long." They crossed

California and Paint creeks, which had steep banks. Two nights out the soldiers camped near Flat Top. It was cold and one could hear the gale, but above this soon was heard a tramping and heavy jarring. The Indians under Quanah had stampeded the buffalo. They were making directly for the sleeping camp. There was no time to lose, but the men acted promptly, and the immense herds of brown animals were turned off by the waving of blankets, and were soon seen thundering off in the night down the banks to the flats below the camp, awakening every sleeper.

The camp moved early toward Duck Creek, and the trail toward Quanah led over a rolling prairie, thinly covered with mesquite and prairie dogs. It was here that the two infantry groups were left to guard, and it was Mackenzie's intention to strike out at night and make a quick march, surprising the enemy. After some time, they found themselves in a small box canyon or break, and by a hard march found themselves near the Freshwater Fork of the Brazos River. The country was rough with some foothills and small arroyos. Frequent halts were made, and it was dark when they were ready to go into camp. It could be described as a "pocket valley." They were in a narrow pocket, with a line of small bluffs or foothills close on either side, and a quicksand stream on the other.

Of course, the soldiers posted pickets. It was near midnight. All was still except for the noises of the horses grazing. The fires had been allowed to die down, and all was dark, when suddenly a yell from the lips of Quanah's Indians rang down the valley. Many more bloodcurdling yells, a sound of shots — and the camp was attacked. The ridge of foothills was alive with Indians, riding at full speed, shaking dried buffalo robes, ringing bells, yelling like wild demons, and in every possible way trying to stampede the animals. Everything was confusion, and above all this din of arms could be heard the yells and cries and shouts of Indians and soldiers with 600 horses and mules rearing, jumping, plunging, running, and snorting with terror and fear. The Indians had found the white soldiers who had gone out to find them. The Indians took about seventy-five of the best horses.

Several of the soldiers who were sent out to round up some of the horses, were soon surrounded by the Indians. The Indians were poorly armed with muzzle-loading rifles and pistols, lances, and bows. They tried to move to the rear, and several of the men were struck. Quanah at this time led the group of Indians on a coal-black racing pony. Leaning forward upon his mane, his heels nervously working in the animal's side, with six-shooter poised in air, he was the incarnation of a savage. His face was smeared with black war paint, which gave his features a hard, cruel look. A full-length headdress of eagle feathers spread out as he rode, and descended from his forehead over the head and back, almost sweeping the ground. He wore large brass hoops in his ears, and was naked to his waist, wearing leggings, moccasins, and a breechcloth. A necklace of bear's claws hung about his neck. His scalp lock was carefully braided in with otter fur, and tied with bright red flannel. His horse's bridle was ornamented with bits of silver, and red flannel was also braided in his mane and tail; but being black, he was not painted. Bells jingled as he rode at a fast speed, followed by his warriors, all eager to take the lead. This was Quanah, the chief of the Quahadas. After killing one of the soldiers by the name of Gregg, the Indians suddenly turned and followed their leader without waiting to pursue the other white men. He had seen the Tonkawa Indians coming in the distance, and he did not want to be caught or pressed between the ravine and the mountains with no chance to escape.

The troopers by this time had come upon the scene, and

they moved toward the flying Comanches pushing toward the butte of *Cañon Blanco*. In the rear of the Indian lines, the squaws were bringing up the ponies, keeping up the shrill screeching and screaming; and at the base of the butte, the Indians were spread out two or three hundred strong, moving about. Every individual warrior kept in constant and continual motion, fighting for himself. Upon the sides of the mountain, the Indians could be seen gliding from rock to rock as their line fell back. The deep arroyos and ravines were full of Indians, circling, firing, and falling back. They had no idea of being caught in any traps, and the rapid movement of the galloping soldiers hastened their steps.

The Indians were being continually mounted on fresh horses, while those of the soldiers were worn by the marches, the stampede, and the hard run of that morning. The Indians held the white soldiers off as long as they could, so that the women and children could escape, then they fled on their horses to the plains. The last Quahada rapidly disappeared in the hills and ravines and ascended to the plateau of the Staked Plains.

The two groups of soldiers then separated. Lieutenant C. A. Vernon went back with the dismounted men who had lost their horses. The other group went on for the trail of the Comanche village. They marched all the following day without catching even a glimpse of an Indian. These had folded their tents and silently stolen away. There was a long delay in scaling a steep ascent with horses, but after toiling over many rocky bluffs, they came out into a vast expanse of prairie. It stretched out in a large plain, and this was the expanse over which the soldiers would trail Quanah's moving village.

It was now October 12 and a cold, overcast gray morning. The air was cold and a severe "norther" began to strike this wasteland. Without the Indian guides the soldiers would have been lost and abandoned the tasks, for the Comanches cleverly foiled the trail by turning back. They estimated that the Comanches had from two to three hundred head of stock that they were moving with the entire village. But the bitter cold increased and, with no shelter and no overcoats, the suffering was intense for the soldiers. The trail grew fresher and warmer. They could observe in the distance silhouetted figures moving against the skyline. They were the Comanches.

The afternoon was almost gone, and ahead was the dark, moving mass of the fleeing village. The Comanches tried to swarm about the flanks of the soldiers. Then the rangers came upon the fires still burning, which the Indians had hastily abandoned upon the approach of the soldiers. There were the lodge-poles scattered in many large numbers on the trail in their sudden flight, and many iron and stone hammers, mortars, and all sorts of strange tools. Puppy dogs of the Indian half-wolf breed had been dropped by the squaws. Great chunks of mulberry wood and mesquite roots were all along, and occasionally the dried buffalo skins of their teepees or lodges. The chase had grown hot. The dark cloud of fleeing Indians was now close at hand. Still the braves dashed and circled about, watching for a chance to attack the column of soldiers. But it was growing dark and cold. The air grew more hazy, and soon there was a cold rain, and sleet and snow. This was the crisis.

If the soldiers had speeded up, made a sharp dash among the frightened women and children, the entire village would have been destroyed. But Mackenzie never gave the order to go forward. The village, which seemed but a mile or more away, was at once shut from the view of the soldiers. The horses were thin and very much worn, and the Indians had fresh mounts. The men were tired and fagged, but all they needed was the word to "turn loose," and finish the Indians then and there, for they had come many miles to accomplish this. No one knows Mackenzie's thoughts at that moment or whether his judgment was best.

A black curtain of night fell, and the norther shut out the fleeing village and saved them. It was more than three years later that the half-breed Quanah was driven to the Fort Sill reservation. Mackenzie had the soldiers dismount when the storm broke with fury. The rain and wind froze the clothes of the men, and the wind increased to a gale. The men were lost going just 500 yards away. Hailstones began to fall, pelting the animals, so that it was difficult for the men to hold them.

The next day, the storm was spent, and there was sunshine, but the spirits of the soldiers had waned, for there was no living creature in sight on the vast prairie. The village had been moving all night, and the chase now looked hopeless. The nearest post was Fort Sumner in New Mexico. The horses of the soldiers were suffering with cold and beginning to show signs of giving out. The food was growing slim. The Comanches had a night's march ahead of the men.

So Mackenzie turned back. The men had nothing to cook the food with but buffalo chips, and a little water to drink. On the first day's march back, the men picked up hundreds of smooth, well-worn cedar lodge-poles which the Comanches had dropped in their flight. The soldiers used these for fuel.

Taking the same route back, there was nothing to relieve the march. They arrived again in Blanco Canyon. Some of the soldiers' horses died, and others too weak to move had to be shot down. Rations and forage for the horses arrived. Mackenzie felt that Quanah, thinking that the soldiers had abandoned pursuit, would turn back from the Pecos River and move to one of his old, well-known haunts on the Pease

River. Determined, he divided the command and sent all those disabled, dismounted men and weak, sick animals into Duck Creek. On October 24, Mackenzie's wound proved too painful, and he was compelled to join the other group. It was with great caution, intense cold, and much suffering that they made their way across the California and Paint Creeks and the Clear Fork of the Brazos, and slowly reached Fort Griffin on November 12. On November 17, they continued on toward Fort Richardson, where another storm broke with driving sleet and ice. They were compelled to go into camp. The men tried to save the animals from perishing by using the saddles and blankets for covers. Breaking camp in the midst of the raging storm, with the snow from six to eight inches deep, the entire command staggered into the protection of the post-oak timber, and were soon pushing on to Fort Richardson, tired out, cold, hungry, and dirty, having been gone since May 1st.

From this Battle of Blanco Canyon, it can be seen that the Quahada Indians were noted for their bravery and close fighting. But General Mackenzie was not to be easily discouraged, for the Indians were still stealing horses in northern Texas. In 1872, he took 272 men and set out following almost the same path he had taken the year before. He found the Comanches on McClellan Creek, north of the Red River, on Sept. 29, 1872. This was not the group that had Quanah for their leader, but those under chief Mowwis. There was a battle, in which twenty warriors were killed and 130 women were captured, and a herd of some 3000 horses taken. They burned the camp. This was a hard blow for the Comanche tribe.

With this many women and children captive, the forays were somewhat checked, and it was not until June of 1873 that the women and children of the Comanches were returned to their people at Fort Sill, on the condition that

there would be no more violence. But they continued with
their raids. The frontier had become a battleground after
the Civil War had ceased. The Indians would kill the
whites, and the whites would kill the Indians. The majority
of the Kiowas, Comanches, and Apaches were constantly off
their reservations at Fort Sill. The Southern Plains tribes
continued their raiding and stealing.

During this time, it is known that Quanah was one of
the sub-chiefs and married the daughter of Yellow Bear, another chief. Quanah made one last desperate effort to hold
his Indians together, and through his influence and wily di-
plomacy succeeded in persuading all the bands of the Comanche and Cheyenne tribes, some of the Kiowas and other
Indians, to affiliate with him in attacking the whites. In
1847, the Comanches held a tribal medicine dance, and in-
vited these other tribes to come. This was held at the mouth
of the Elk Creek and the north fork of the Red River. On
the site of the old Bent's Fort at Bent's Creek, the Indians
gathered, and Quanah was the leader of the Quahadas. He
urged the Indians to attack a well-organized company of
white buffalo hunters who (he claimed) were depredating
upon the well-recognized Indian lands over which the immense herds of buffalo grazed. The Indians relied on these
animals for almost their very existence in houses, (skins
for lodges), clothing, food, etc. Thus, he mustered about 700
warriors, and the campaign began June 24, 1874. Led by
Quanah, himself, with his confederate Indians and his friend
Big Bow of another tribe of Comanches, they attacked these
hunters who were entrenched in a rude fort known as the
Adobe Walls. There had been some settlement here, and a
trading post and headquarters for buffalo hunters.

Adobe Wall Creek is in the present Hutchinson County,
Texas, and flows south into the Canadian in the Texas panhandle. The new buildings stood two miles above its mouth.

The old Bent's Post had crumbled into ruins, and there now were two stores, a saloon, and a blacksmith shop. The white people had grown careless on this warm summer day, and they did not think of such a large group of Indians gathering to attack them. But in addition to the thick walls, the hunters had a small field piece which they could use with good effect.

With a mighty war whoop and all kinds of noise and paint on their bodies, these Indians fell on the settlement. It was almost thirty minutes after the first attack when they finally drew off, and they killed some of the white frontiersmen. The others boarded themselves behind the protecting walls of one of the buildings, and started to kill the Indians with their rifle fire. After a siege lasting all day, the Indians were obliged to withdraw with considerable loss. But they came back the second and the third day, to suffer additional losses. The Indians finally realized that they were no match for the guns of the white man, and instead of carrying the attack and the war on from the Rio Grande to the Dakotas, they rode back to their reservation at Fort Sill. Quanah was beginning to realize now that the Indian must submit to the superior force of the white man. They made their camp on the plains, but water was scarce in the year of 1875.

The leaders in Washington felt that force must be used upon the Indians, and so, four groups of men were selected to converge in columns upon them, surround them, and bring them into submission. Quanah was implacable to the last, but these four converging columns finally administered the death blow to him and his legions. Four commands came from four directions: General Nelson A. Miles from Camp Supply, Colonel R. S. MacKenzie from Fort Griffin, another group from Fort Sill, which was at the mouth of Wanderer's Creek on the Red River, and Major Price from

New Mexico was to come eastward from Ft. Union. The Comanche must choose submission or destruction, and Quanah began to lead his people to the reservation.

CHAPTER XIII

Quanah on the Reservation

THE REMNANTS of the Comanche tribes were gathered on their reservation around Fort Sill in 1875. The Indian reservation is located on the Comanche, Kiowa, and Apache lands. It is 123 miles north of Fort Richardson, about 190 miles southwest of Camp Supply, thirty miles south of Washita, and forty-five miles north of the Red River. The site was selected by General Sheridan in his winter campaign of 1868-9, and for many years served as a base of operations against the confederated tribes of Comanches, Kiowas, Southern Cheyennes, and Arapahoes. It was occupied by General Grierson with the 10th Cavalry in June, 1868, under the name of Camp Wichita, although it had been known for a short time previous as Camp Sheridan. It was occupied as a post in January 1869, but the name was changed to Fort Sill on August 1, 1869, by General Sheridan, in memory of General J. W. Sill, who was killed at the Battle of Stone's River, December 31, 1862.

The reservation is in the form of a quadrangle, nine miles in length by four in width. Within its boundaries are the Cache and Medicine Bluff creeks, at the junction of

which is located the post. This area is about one square mile
in the center of the military reservation. It is on a plateau of
irregular outline sloping in all directions. The Witchita
Mountains are in plain sight and extend from the northwest corner of the reservation westward about fifty miles.
They give a grandeur and beauty to the entire country. A
network of streams rises in these mountains. Mesquite, oak,
and hackberry abound. Buffalo, elk, bear, antelope, white-
tailed deer, panthers, wolves, jackrabbits, wildcats, otter,
prairie dogs, and raccoons were abundant. Trout, bass, and
many kinds of fish have been found. Buffalo swarmed the
prairies, and quail and highland plover were killed in incredible numbers.

To the Indians, the buffalo was the staff of life. It was
their food, clothing, dwelling, and tools. It is not strange
then that the animal was reverenced by them. The robe was
the Indian's covering and his bed, while the skin, dressed, was
his blanket. The hide was used for moccasins, leggings, shirts,
and clothes for the women. The dressed cowhides were used
for their lodges, and were warm and comfortable. Braided
strands of rawhide furnished them with lariats and lines, as
did the twisted hair. The green hide was sometimes used as
a kettle in which to boil meat. The tough, thick hide of the
bull's neck, after it had shrunk smooth, made a shield for
the men. From the rawhide, they made bags to carry their
belongings. The bones and ribs were made into rough tools
for scraping and dressing the hides, and the shoulder blades
made hoes and axes. The hoofs were boiled to make glue
for fastening the feathers and heads on their arrows. The
horns furnished spoons and ladles, and ornamented the war
bonnets. Water vessels were made from the lining of the
paunch. Knife sheaths, bow cases, gun covers, saddle cloths,
and pouches were furnished by the buffalo. The buffalo
hunt was the main event of the year, but after a few years

they found no buffalo herds and no meat, and Quanah realized that the old life was over and they would have to live on the white man's food, for they had no buffalo meat and no skins to make clothes. The old Indian life was truly gone, and the ways of the white man had come.

They still made meat their main diet, but there were many facets of civilization which were strange to them. Every two weeks, they received an issue of rations. The scene in and about the commissary on these days defies description. There were all varieties of robes, skins, and blankets of red, green, and various colors. Flour, bacon, sugar sacks, pans, kettles and unnameable stuff was scattered all over the grounds. The squaws' shrill voices, the half-breed wolf-dogs, barking, snarling, and howling, the papooses' heads showing over the tops of the blankets of the cradles around which they had been wrapped, the beadlike black eyes always roving about only to dodge down again if watched, was a sight to behold. All were yelling or howling in chorus, the loud laughter of the Indian braves making a babel of voices and noises. The ration issue was begun inside the building, and a chief representing so many families or lodges stepped up, upon the calling of his name, and handed the clerk a card, which told the clerk how many persons were drawing the rations. The clerk entered the amount into the books, and the men shoveled out the coffee, sugar and flour, and weighed out the bacon or pork. These supplies were in great bins, and this was repeated until all the families of the various bands were given their allotted amount.

When it was over, the squaws did the packing, lashing, and driving of the mules. The half-breed dogs were expressing their joy by barks and yelps, and the warriors were mounting their horses. Then, after a scene of confusion and pandemonium, the Indian village was on the move again. There were pack mules and dogs of all breeds, shades, sizes, degrees; and squaws who were old, as well as many young girls. The women dressed so much like the warriors that it was hard to distinguish them from the men. They did wear their moccasins higher, with a long legging, and with a half-skirt of buckskin or dirty calico with a half-apron in front. They were all unkempt, dirty, wretched, squalid, and alive with vermin. And, with confusion and ear-splitting noises, they finally streamed over the prairie back to their lodges on the plateau. Their reservation was beautiful and had rich grass and many streams for water. There was some sickness, and malaria was not uncommon. Quanah had seen enough during these years to fear the white man less than the average Indian did. He seemed to have one desire, and that was to find his mother's people. According to some books, the Indian agent at Fort Sill gave him a letter, with which he started out to east Texas in search of his mother's people. It is believed that he found his mother's brother, Silas; one of the children who had not been taken captive when Cynthia Ann was taken by the Indians. Silas was grown and married, and had built himself a log cabin in Van Zandt County. It was to this home that Quanah went. It must have been very strange to Quanah to picture his mother; the ways of the white man are hard for the Indian to understand.

After making this visit, he returned to the Indian reservation at Fort Sill in time for the buffalo hunt. He found that, while he was gone, there had been trouble in getting the Indians to fill the rolls of the Indian police and school. Therefore no permission was granted for the buffalo hunt until there were enough Indians to take part in this program. Having satisfied this requirement, they went to the plains and tried to find the buffalo, but they failed and it was with heavy heart that the last group of Comanche war-

riors reached the reservation with no meat and no hides for the winter.

Quanah had several wives beside Weckeah. They were Chony, Mahcheetowooky, and Aewithtakum; and some of the children were named Naunocca and Woonardy, Baldwin, White, and Laura. It was difficult to follow the white man's ways when it came to the matter of family life, and until his death he had several wives. He loved each one very dearly and cared for them well on his reservation.

Because of the suitability of the prairie lands for grazing, he was much sought after by the cattlemen of Texas and Oklahoma. He had many transactions with S. B. Burnett of Fort Worth, to whom he leased the grazing lands of his tribes for $100,000 per annum. This he distributed among his people. He found another friend in Dan Wagoner. They invited him to the Stock Show at Fort Worth, which was held every year, and he enjoyed this very much. It was on one of these trips to Fort Worth that he learned he could place an advertisement asking if anyone had a picture of his mother. He did not understand how a picture could be taken, but, on the advice of a friend, he said that if anyone knew of a picture, he would like to obtain this photograph. Captain Sul Ross, who led the Rangers at the time of the capture of Cynthia Ann, saw the advertisement. He lived in Waco at that time, and knowing that a picture had been made of Cynthia Ann Parker, he secured one and had it sent to Quanah. Quanah's joy and happiness at seeing the face of his mother was more than he could understand. He knew that she had been gone from him these many years, and that she had died soon after the white people had taken her away from him. She was dressed as a white woman, and her hair was cut short, and the little sister was in her arms. This was one of the happiest experiences of his life, and he treasured it.

Quanah was the principal chief of the Comanches. He spoke English well, wore a fine suit and shoes, a hat and a necktie. But he kept his long hair in braids. He annually went to Fort Worth. He traveled as far as New Orleans and saw the World's Fair in 1885. He went to Washington and visited President Cleveland, and saw the impressive sights of the capitol city. It was a long cry from the lodges on the banks of the river to the large cities of the East.

In 1886, he and Yellow Bear, who was the father of his beloved wife, Weckeah, went to Fort Worth to the Stock Show. But tragedy fell upon them, for Yellow Bear, unaccustomed to modern ways, blew out the gas when he went to bed, instead of turning it off. Quanah came in and retired. He said later that he noticed a strange sweet smell, but did not become alarmed about it. The next morning both Indians were found unconscious. Quickly they saw that Yellow Bear was dead, but Quanah was still breathing and had a little pulse. After working over him, Quanah was revived, but he made a sad journey back to his people with the body of his friend Yellow Bear. It is fortunate that one of them was spared, for the Indians might have thought that it was done purposely by the white people.

Some books on Quanah say that he is the one responsible for bringing the "peyote" weed to the Indians. They claim that he went to see his mother's brother John, who was at that time living on the Rio Grande, and that he brought it back with him. The Indians called it "hoas" or "hose." It was dangerous, and the agents tried to keep the Indians from obtaining this weed. It could have been brought back from earlier raids along the Rio Grande, or sent in with the Mexican traders. Finally, by the persuasion of the white leaders, they limited its use to the ceremonial festivals of the new moon.

Quanah's position increased in importance when he was

made one of the members of the Court of Indian Offenses, which met to judge the cases of the Indians on the reservation. Two other men, Lone Wolf, a Kiowa, and Jim Tehuacana, made the hearings more impartial. They met twice a month, and Quanah was the presiding judge, receiving a small amount of money for his services. Since he had acquired some wealth also from leasing the ranges, his friend Burnett finally persuaded Quanah to let him build a house for him. This was a large square building with a two-story porch around the three sides. On the fourth side, a one-story wing was added, with a porch and a larger dining room and kitchen. The main part had six rooms downstairs, and four above. It was painted white with a red roof, and there was a large white star which decorated each side of the square roof. He bought many things of the white men, such as chairs, tables, beds, stoves, and other furnishings.

When the children of these Indians were seven or eight years old, they were sent to Indian schools at the agency, which was a government school, or at Carlisle, Pennsylvania. One of Quanah's daughters, Patsi, was sent to Carlisle, when she was five, to learn the white men's ways. Strange indeed that Cynthia Ann's grandchild was taken to the white man to learn their ways, when Cynthia Ann herself had been taken away as a child of nine to learn the Indian life. Many of the Comanche children went to Carlisle, but a new school was started at Chilocco in 1884.

For the most part, the Indians were unsettled and miserable. It is true that every two weeks they were given sugar, flour, rice, and other staple crops. They had beef given to them also. But the young men were restless, for they could not be warriors like their fathers, or work for wages as did the white man. They received a little money from the leasing of the pastures for grass to the cattlemen.

But when it was divided among them, it anmounted to from two to five cents per acre. When it was time for the new leases to be made, some of the tribal council wanted to renew them, but others refused to do this. Since the decision had to be made in Washington, they decided to send some of the Indians to the capital. Quanah was chosen by the Comanches, Whiteman by the Apaches, and Lone Wolf by the Kiowas. George Day, who was the agent, went with them. The opposition also sent a group composed of White Wolf and Tabbynanaka, and Sunboy of the Kiowas, and two white men, Thomas Woodward and G. W. Conover. It was decided to lease the lands. While there, they were formally met by President Harrison, and came on home to receive the grass money. The cattlemen who leased the grass were good friends of Quanah, and two of his daughters married these cattlemen. Emmet Cox married Nau-nocca Parker, and A. G. Birdsong married Laura Neda Parker.

In 1896, Quanah made another trip to Washington. His wife, Tonarcy, went with him, and they stopped at Carlisle, where three of his children were attending school. The thirty years set by the Treaty of Medicine Lodge for the issuing of rations ended in 1897. At this time, most of the Indians had cattle and were raising crops on their farms. They still had some payments of their grass money. But the Indians were fearful that the white men would take these lands away from them.

It was just after the Spanish-American War had been finished that the famous Teddy Roosevelt held a reunion of his Rough Riders in Oklahoma City, and Quanah was asked to bring a troop of Indians for the celebration. There he met Theodore Roosevelt and was pleased with his spirit and understanding. He liked the president at once, and their friendship continued.

Again a new agreement caused trouble among the Indians over their lands. This plan was made without much thought for the Indians, and was called the Jerome agreement. It had been presented six years before, and the Indians had talked it down. Therefore, when it was proposed again, Quanah made another trip to Washington and talked with President McKinley. President McKinley assured him that the allotments were necessary, and that the Indians would receive only 160 acres. Quanah felt that this was not enough, and that the Indians should have at least 300 acres. He reminded the president that, at one time, it had all belonged to them. He was embittered, and felt that this president had treated him unfairly.

The land, which the Indians had, would be disposed of in this fashion. In this case, instead of the run which had been used to distribute the land previously, each claim had to be registered. Then all the names were put in a great wheel and drawn out one by one. Persons could then choose their claims in the order that their names were drawn. In a few weeks, the lands had been given out, and the Comanche country was full of white settlers, plowing and building homes. Three townsites — Lawton, Hobart and Anadarko — were laid out, the last site being the location of the Kiowa-Comanche agency.

With the settlers came the missionaries, and nearest Quanah's home was a Methodist mission at the sub-agency south of Fort Sill. It was at this sub-agency that the Comanches received their rations. There was a Baptist mission a few miles north. White Parker, son of Quanah, educated at Carlisle, became a Methodist minister. There was also a Mennonite mission called Post Oak Mission. Rev. Mr. Becker and the family of Quanah became good friends.

Because he could not be still, and restlessness was upon him, he traveled a great deal. One of his daughters went with him to the World's Fair at Chicago. In 1906, he went to the national renunion of the Sons of the Confederate Veterans at New Orleans. In March, after the death of President McKinley, he went to see the inauguration of President Roosevelt. But the pressure of the white people for more land led to the passing of another bill, opening the sale of the reserved pasture and woodlands in March, 1906. All children born in the tribes since 1901 received allotments in the pasture lands. December 3 was the date set for the land office commissioners to begin opening the bids and awarding claims to the new purchasers. On November 16, 1907, the admission of the new state of Oklahoma was approved.

In 1909, Quanah had the pleasure of seeing the daughter of his mother's brother, whose name was Bessie Parker St. John, wife of John P. St. John, a notable governor of Kansas. In one of her letters, she writes that Quanah's home was on a creek near the southern slope of the Wichita Mountains. Quanah had married eight times, but only three of his wives were living. Mrs. St. John says he was a fine specimen of physical manhood, tall, muscular, and as straight as an arrow. He looked you straight in the eye; had dark skin, perfect teeth, and heavy, raven black hair. He wore it hanging in two rolls wrapped around with a red cloth. His hair was parted in the middle, while the scalplock was a portion of hair the size of a dollar, plaited and tangled, signifying: If you want a fight, you can have it.

Quanah visited Roosevelt again and was entertained in the Blue Room. A group of white men and Indians had taken pictures of a catching of the wolf in a wolf-hunt, and a mock attack of the town of Cache. These pictures were shown to Roosevelt and to his guests, with the delighted Quanah present. Roosevelt's appreciation of him helped Quanah reconcile his bitterness toward the white man, for he knew that Roosevelt was a powerful leader of the white men, and the big chief.

Quanah died February 22, 1911, of an attack of asthma and rheumatism. He left three wives and fifteen children. He was reputed to be the wealthiest Indian in the United States. He was buried at Post Oak Mission Cemetery, near Lawton, on February 24, 1911. At sunrise on the morning of his death, the real Indian burial ceremony began. Three times during the night, Tonarcy, the favorite of Quanah's three remaining wives, called to the Great Spirit for her chief. At five o'clock, she waked all the family, and said, "This is the time I always build a fire for him." At six o'clock, the Chief Medicine Man of the tribe conducted the sunrise funeral, crying to the Great Spirit and to the white man's god to accept the spirit of the dead chief. The Indians chanted weird dirges. More than 1000 persons attended, including hundreds of Indians.

The body of Quanah was dressed in his buckskin suit of former days. At noon the funeral party wended its way among the hills of the Parker ranch to the little Indian cemetery, and the funeral service began. Rev. Becker, the Mennonite missionary friend, conducted the service. Following this, the Indians sang the Swan Song, the Medicine Man again cried to the Great Spirit, and the body was lowered to the side of his white mother. In the coffin were placed a buckskin bag containing Quanah's favorite feathers, his war bonnet, trinkets, and jewelry. Among the latter was a diamond brooch, valued at $450, the present of cattlemen who had grazed their stock on the Comanche ranges fifteen years before. When Quanah died, there were only about 1500 of his Comanche tribe left. The Comanche trail had become a state, and the white man had driven the Indians to their reservation with little hope for the future generations.

CHAPTER XIV

Cynthia Ann's Monuments and Landmarks of Today

WHEN IT WAS FIRST learned that there was a movement to transfer the body of Cynthia Ann Parker to the Indian reservation in Oklahoma, there was a storm of protest. It was Cynthia Ann's son, Quanah Parker, who was desirous of having his mother's body brought to Oklahoma to be with her Indian people. This was forty-five years after her death, and the white men threatened to protect the grove where she was buried, with guns. But the impassioned plea that Quanah, the Indian son, be allowed to bury his mother, awakened a sympathetic response throughout the civilized world.

The following is said to be a letter that was read before some of the churches in east Texas, where the opposition was so strong; this letter was written by Quanah Parker from his home in Cache, Oklahoma:

My mother. She fed me. She held me. She carried me in her arms. Her boy. See me, she happy, I play, she happy.

I cry, she sad. I laugh, her eyes shine. I sleepy, she roll my blanket, she pat me. I sick, she awake. I thirsty, she get water; she not tired, not deep sleeping, not cross, her boy. He want, she get. Laugh with boy, cry with boy. Love boy, my mother. Love mother. Don't say Indian, say boy. They took my mother away. They kept her. They would not let me see her. Now she dead. Her boy want to bury her. Sit by her mound. My people. Her people. Our people. We now one, all our people. Comanches had much land. Sunrise, sunset, broad grasslands, buffalo, deer, wild horses, now little land. No more Texas. Few Indians, little land. Lonesome. White brothers, boy bury mother, my mother. She mine. Me bury her, you keep her, she mine. Her dust, my dust. White brothers, your mother, you bury. My mother, I boy. Her dust, I bury. I sit on her mound. Love mother Boy plead. My mother.[1]

After this plea was read at the little church in Anderson County by a missionary preacher, real opposition was withdrawn, and the white relatives finally gave their consent. It was forty-five years after her death, and the Congress of the United States, by act of March 5, 1909, (Statutes 35, page 802) states: "For a monument to Cynthia Ann Parker, mother of Quanah Parker, chief of the Comanches, one thousand dollars to be expended under such regulations as the secretary of the Interior may prescribe." Then in June 25, 1910, Congress (Statutes 36, p. 797) authorizes an expenditure for removing the remains of Cynthia Ann Parker and her daughter from Texas to Cache, Oklahoma: "The Secretary of the Interior is authorized to use out of the sum of $1,000 appropriated in the act approved March 3, 1909 for a monument to Cynthia Parker not exceeding 200 dollars for necessary expenses of removing from Texas and reinterring in Oklahoma the bodies of said Cynthia Ann Parker and her daughter, Prairie Flower."

---

[1] Ralph Selle, *Here Comes Texas*, pp. 16, 17.

Chief Quanah Parker exhumed the body of his mother and reburied her in December of 1910 in the Post Oak Cemetery near Cache, Oklahoma. Cache is about fifteen miles west of Lawton and halfway between Snyder and Lawton, Oklahoma. It was not long after this that Quanah himself was buried beside his mother, on Feb. 23, 1911. On May 30, 1930, another monument was placed beside that of his mother, Cynthia Ann. This money was appropriated by Congress, and this was for Quanah Parker. The inscription written by his daughter, Neda Parker Birdsong, is as follows:

QUANAH PARKER

The Last Chief of the Comanches
B 1852   D. Feb. 23, 1911
Resting here until the day breaks
and the shadows fall and darkness
disappears.

Thus, Quanah and his mother Cynthia Ann rest in the midst of the reservation of their Comanche people, a symbol of the blending of the red people and the white people into the Americans of today.

Fort Parker State Park. On May 5, 1936, the year of the Texas Centennial Celebrations, the Mexia Lumber Mills Company of the city of Mexia was given a contract by the State of Texas to erect a log replica of old Fort Parker for the price of $8,422. A second unit was to be a smokehouse by the side of the fort. On May 19, 1936, a centennial observance was held of the 100 years since the erection of Fort Parker, and the massacre there by the Comanche and Kiowa Indians. On May 19, 1936, many people gathered near the present town of Groesbeck, and the first logs were laid that day at the fort site in the construction of a replica of the old stockade and cabins. The date was a famous one, for it was on May 19 that the massacre and attack of the Indians occurred, and Cynthia Ann and her brother John, and two of the other white woman of the stockade, were captured by the red men. The buildings now stand completed on the unfenced prairie, just as they did 100 years ago in May, when other walls echoed the weird calls of savages and the cries of the Parker settlers as they were killed and captured. Every effort was made to have each detail of the original fort duplicated in the present structure.

The garden has been planted with vegetables, and one of the cabins furnished with pioneer tools and home implements. In the middle of the stockade, by the flagpole, was the grave of Cynthia Ann's grandfather, Elder John Parker, who was seventy-nine years old when he was killed. Here, within an area of 1700 acres, stands this reproduction of old Fort Parker. The replica of the original fort can now be seen. The State Park was opened officially May 1, 1941, in memory of the Parker family who first located on this ground in 1836. There is a 750-acre lake created by a dam across the Navasota River. The granite marker to the memory of John Parker, as a shrine to his courage and faith, was unveiled August 10, 1946.

Cynthia Ann Hotel. About eight miles south of Fort Parker in the city of Groesbeck, Texas, is this hotel, named in memory of Cynthia Ann.

Crowell, Texas. There was a marker unveiled on the courthouse square in memory of Cynthia Ann Parker, on April 27, 1936. It was near Crowell, Texas, that Cynthia Ann was captured by the white soldiers. Turn right from Crowell on State Highway 283 to a junction with a dirt road five and one-half miles; go right here past the city of Margaret, which is a town of 200 population, a farming community with a few stores, ten and one-half miles to the site of the recapture of Cynthia Parker, twelve and one-half miles away. Here, on December 18, 1860, took place a skirmish between the Rangers under the command of Captain L. S. Ross, and a band of Comanches under Peta Nocona, which resulted in the death of the war chief and the rescue of his wife, Cynthia Ann Parker, who had been captured by the Comanches in 1836. A daughter, Prairie Flower, was captured with her, but her two sons escaped.

Cache, Oklahoma. This town is on the old Comanche Indian reservation, and is about fifteen miles west of Lawton and fifteen miles east of Snyder, with a population of only about 677 people. Two monuments are there side by side, one for Quanah Parker and the other for Cynthia Ann Parker, on the Post Oak Mission Cemetery lots.

Isaac Parker's house, Fort Worth, Texas. When Cynthia Ann was recaptured and taken to Birdsville by her uncle, Isaac Parker, she lived in the home in 1860. In April 22, 1939, Amon G. Carter moved the house from its original location in Birdsville and completely restored it in a natural setting at his Shady Oaks Farm near Lake Worth. This was in commemoration of Cynthia Ann and was called "Cynthia Ann's House." Every log is in its place, just as it was when Cynthia Ann took up her residence there in 1860. Even the old rail fence has been erected, and an ancient farm wagon moved with the house to complete the picture.

Antelope Hills, Texas. These are in northern Shackelford County, west of old Fort Griffin, averaging slightly more than 1500 feet. This is the location of the famous battle of Antelope Hills.

Comanche, Texas. This town in Texas was established in 1858, when John Duncan offered Comanche County 240 acres on Indian Creek near the center of the county as a site for a county seat. The first courthouse was a picket house of logs cut and split on the ground, set vertically in a ditch and covered with boards, but was named for the Comanche Indians who roamed this county.

Comanche County. In West Central Texas, this county comprises an area of 972 square miles, with level to rolling, partly broken terrain. Although the Comanche County area was included in the Mexican government's grant to Stephen F. Austin and Samuel May Williams, no settlement was made until 1854 when four families moved in from Williamson County. By late 1855, thirty or forty families had arrived. The county was created in 1856 from Coryell and Bosque counties, and was named for the Comanche Indians.

Comanche Creek. At least eight Texas streams are known as Comanche Creek, and are in the following counties showing the extent of the Comanche influence: 1. Anderson County. 2. Bexar County. 3. Blanco County. 4. Mason County. 5. Maverick County. 6. Pecos County. 7. San Saba County. 8. Uvalde County.

Comanche Springs, Texas. These are at the headwaters of Comanche Creek at the town of Fort Stockton in Pecos County, well-known to the Indians and to the early explorers of Texas. According to legend, the spring was named by a group of hunters who one night shot at what they thought was a wolf, near the edge of the camp. At daybreak, the hunters found a Comanche Indian in a wolfskin, and from this incident the springs are said to have been named.

Comanche Trail. This is an elusive reference, but a map of West Texas, by J. H. Young in 1857, shows such a trail. The lower part had two prongs, one crossing the Rio Grande about the vicinity of Boquillas, and the other at Presidio, and the two converging at Comanche Springs near the present sight of Fort Stockton. From this point the trail extended north to Big Springs. There were two routes across the Staked Plains. One was up Yellow House Canyon by Buffalo Springs to the forks of the canyon and then to the north fork of the Brazos where Abernathy is now, and on to Sod House Spring north of the present Littlefield. From here, one went to Pecos, near old Fort Sumner; the other route extended southeast to Blanco Canyon and up that canyon past Plainview and then west to Spring Lake. From Spring Lake it continued to the present site of Muleshoe.

Comanche Peak. At least two Texas elevations are known as Comanche Peak. The first is in El Paso County three miles north of El Paso, rising to an elevation of 5220 feet. The other Comanche Peak is between Tolar and Fort Spunky, with an elevation of 1300 feet.

Nocona, Texas. A town named after Quanah's father and the Indian chief Peta Nocona, the husband of Cynthia Ann Parker. It is on the M.K.&T.R.R. in Montague County, a few miles south of the old Spanish Fort on the Red River.

Quanah, Texas. This is a town in the Texas panhandle, some miles east of Canyon Blanco, the county seat of Hardeman County. It is not far from the town of Vernon. This town of Quanah is named for the Comanche Indian chief, and is near the location where Peta Nocona, his father, was killed, and where his mother was recaptured by Captain Ross' Rangers. It is in the center of the county between the Red and the Pease rivers, which was the Comanche country. The first town lot sale was held in December, 1886, after the Fort Worth and Denver Railway Co. had made its survey. East of Quanah is Medicine Mound, said to have been the site of religious rites of the Indians. Quanah is the site of the annual Texas-Oklahoma wolf-hunt held on the C. T. Watkins ranch, that became famous during the time of Theodore Roosevelt.

Parker County. In North Central Texas is Parker County, partly on the Grand Prairie and partly in the Western Cross Timbers. The first permanent settlers came to the region after 1849. In December, 1855, the county was created from Bosque and Navarro counties and named for Isaac Parker, representative from the Tarrant district. Isaac Parker moved to a large section of land on the Clear Fork about eight miles east of Weatherford, where he built another log house like the one he had lived in, at Birdsville in 1872. He was the brother of Silas Parker and uncle of Cynthia Ann Parker. He was born in Georgia in 1793. He and Sam Houston fought under General Jackson in the Creek Indian War, and in the charge and slaughter at Horseshoe Bend on the Tallapoosa River. After the close of the war of 1812, which ended with the battle of New Orleans, January 8, 1815, in which Isaac Parker fought, he returned to Tennessee, where he married in 1816, and moved to the wilds of Illinois. He came with the Parkers when they moved to Texas, but did not locate at Fort Parker with the other brothers, James and Silas. Although he was sixty-seven, he could not throw off his warlike spirit, and was again found in the battle line defending the rights of the Confederacy. Mrs. Rebecca Rawlins, the only remaining child of the family, still owns the homesite, and with her husband, Tom Rawlins, lives there. She is a first cousin of Cynthia Ann Parker and has in her possession the buffalo robe worn by Cynthia Ann when she was captured by Sul Ross' men in 1860, and a pair of beaded moccasins which belonged to Chief Quanah Parker. The grave of Isaac Parker, for whom Parker County is named, is on this property, and there is a marker as his monument. He died April 14, 1883, in Parker County.

Descendants of Cynthia Ann Parker. On July 4, 1953, there was a reunion of the white and Indian descendants of Cynthia Ann Parker. One of Quanah's children is named Wanda, and is Mrs. Harry Page of Lawton, Oklahoma. Another daughter is named We-Yo-Dee, and is now seventy years of age. This reunion took place 117 years from the time of the capture of Cynthia Ann by the Comanche Indians. White Parker is a grandson of the famed Cynthia Ann, and a Methodist minister. He has a daughter and a granddaughter, both named Cynthia Ann. His other daughter is called Billie June Topetchez. One of Quanah's sons is named Baldwin Parker, and in 1941 he toured Texas with a program and a play about Cynthia Ann Parker and the Indians. Baldwin Parker has discarded the dress of the red man, but wears his hair in two long braids. His command of English is perfect, and he also speaks Comanche. Baldwin Parker has a granddaughter whose name is also Cynthia Ann III; she is the daughter of Roy Parker.

One of Cynthia Ann's granddaughters, Miss Bertha Parker, was a student nurse at Baylor Hospital on January 18, 1941. Her home is in Lawton, Oklahoma. She is a daughter of White Parker, the grandson of Cynthia Ann. Another great-grandson wed an Indian girl in Waco recently; his name is Baldwin Parker, Jr. Thus it is seen that the influence of Cynthia Ann extends over the state of Texas.

During the Texas Centennial Exposition in 1936, Cynthia Ann Parker, one of the granddaughters, visited the Dallas Fairgrounds. She was ten years old and dressed as an Indian princess. She was the daughter of Mr. and Mrs. White Parker Fletcher, granddaughter of Quanah. Her uncle was Baldwin Parker, who is the leader in the modern Comanche tribe in Oklahoma today. Thus the race is carried on over a period of 100 years, and the fame of Quanah and Cynthia Ann goes on in the hearts of their white and Indian children.

The remains and markers of Cynthia Ann and Quanah Parker have been moved from their resting place at Cache to Fort Sill near Lawton, Oklahoma. The army took over the Comanche lands and extended the military reservation beyond Cache. They have been placed in the cemetery inside of Fort Sill. Today their graves are surrounded by modern buildings and much military activity. The soldiers who pass by every day do not understand what is represented by the two monuments that stand amidst the beautiful flowers. There is little known about these two famous Americans and their important contribution to early Western civilization. They represent the two races that made America great, the red and the white.

The descendants of the Parkers, which includes both races, meet each year on July 4th, alternately at Fort Parker, Texas, or Cache, Oklahoma, in memory of Cynthia Ann and Quanah. The bloodlines are slowly fading away as the generations spread beyond their sacred borders to every state in the Union. There are many Americans in whose veins this blood flows today. They have a rich inheritance that is anchored in the spirit and life of Cynthia Ann and her son, Quanah. Out of the massacre of May 19, 1836, was born the heroine who eventually became the white goddess of the Comanche tribe. Lying in the cemetery of Fort Sill today is the dove of peace that joined the hands of the fierce red man and the conquering white — Cynthia Ann Parker.

Bibliography

Alrich, A. A., *The History of Houston County.*
Batty, Thomas C., *A Quaker Among the Indians.*
Brand, Edward, *Illinois Baptist, a History.*
Brown, A., *Indian Wars and Pioneers.*
Brown, A., *Annals of Travis County.*
Carroll, J. M., *History of Texas Baptists.*
Carter, R. G., *On the Border with Mackenzie.*
De Shields, James T., *Cynthia Ann Parker.*
Dallas Morning News, Aug. 17, 1890, and files in **Library.**
Dictionary of American Biography, IV, 1942.
Elkins, John M., *Indian Fighting on the Texas Frontier.*
Faulk, *Henderson County.*
Hohes, Pauline, *A Centennial History of Anderson County.*
Holland, G. A., *A Double Log Cabin.*
Horton, *Jack County.*
Manning, *History of Van Zandt County.*
Navarro, J., *Henderson Counties.*
Parker, James W., *The Rachel Plummer Narrative.*
Parker, James — Southwestern Microfilm, Inc., *Narrative of Perilous Adventure,* film 35.
Parker, James, *Narration of the Perilous Adventures, Escapes and Sufferings of Rev. James W. Parker.*
Richardson, R. N., *Comanche Barrier to the South Plains Settlement.*
Rister, Carl, *Border Captives.*
———— *Greater Southwest.*
———— *The Southwestern Frontier, 1863-1881.*
Smithwick, Noah, *The Evolution of a State*

Southwestern Historical Quarterly, vol. 46, July 1942.
Texas Almanac, 1936, 1952, 1953.
Texas State Historical Association Quarterly, I, 1897-1898, "Old
      Three Hundred."
Texas State Historical Association, XI-XII, 1907-09. Records of
      an Early Baptist Church.
Tatum, Laurie, *Our Red Brothers in 1899*.
Tilghman, *Quanah*.
Thrall, *History of Texas*.
Wallace, Ernest and Hoebel E. Adamson, *The Comanches, the
      Lords of the South Plains*.
Webb, Walter, *The Handbook of Texas*, vol. I, II.
White, Dabney and Richardson, *East Texas, its History and its
      Markers*, III, 1940.
Wilbarger, J. H., *Indian Depredations in Texas*, 1886.

NEWSPAPERS

Frontier Times
Galveston News
Ft. Worth Gazette
Dallas Morning News

The Author

MRS. GRACE MELVA JACKSON was born in Illinois. She graduated from the University of California at Los Angeles and Berkeley.

Her book CYNTHIA ANN PARKER is the natural outcome of her lifelong interest in the history of American Indians. Apart from her literary exploits, her next best hobby is music, to which she devotes herself in solo and choir directing.

Mrs. Jackson, the wife of Clyde L. Jackson, a minister, was formerly a book reviewer for the Berkeley Gazette. She is a member of Beta Sigma Chi, California Teachers Association, Dallas Teachers Association, and the American Library Association.

www.ingramcontent.com/pod-product-compliance
Lightning Source LLC
Chambersburg PA
CBHW071424150726
48000CB00001B/463